The Yoga Way Cookbook

Natural Vegetarian Recipes

Published by
THE HIMALAYAN INTERNATIONAL INSTITUTE
OF YOGA SCIENCE AND PHILOSOPHY
Honesdale, Pennsylvania

Library of Congress Catalog Card Number: 80-81994

ISBN: 0-89389-067-7

©1980 by the Himalayan International Institute
of Yoga Science and Philosophy

First Edition, 1974
Second Edition, 1975
Third Edition, 1978
Fourth Edition, 1980
Second Printing, 1982

Himalayan International Institute
of Yoga Science and Philosophy of the U.S.A.
RD 1, Box 88
Honesdale, Pennsylvania 18431

Printed in the United States of America

Contents

PRAYER BEFORE MEALS

ॐ ब्रह्मार्पणं ब्रह्महविः
ब्रह्माग्नौ ब्रह्मणा हुतम्।
ब्रह्मैव तेन गन्तव्यं
ब्रह्मकर्म समाधिना।।
ॐ विश्वात्मा प्रीयताम्।

Om Brahmar panam	The offering is to God.
Brahma havih	God is the offering.
Brahma agnau	The offering is made into the fire which is God.
Brahmanu hutam	The offering is made by God.
Brahmaivatena gantavyam	God alone is the one to whom the offering is made.
Brahma karma samadhina	When seen through samadhi, all this action is God.
Om visvatma priyatam	May the Universal Self be satisfied.
Om tat sat. Brahmar panam astu	That alone is true and real. The offering is to God.
Om shantih shantih shantih	Om peace peace peace

O God, bless this food so that it brings vitality and energy to fulfill thy mission and serve humanity.

O God, bless this food so that we remain aware of Thee within and without.

O God, bless this food so that we love all and exclude none.

Bless those who have provided this food, who have prepared this food and who will eat this food.

Bless all, my Lord. Amen.

Something to Know

The body is a sacred vessel, the storehouse of the spirit and the instrument through which the divine manifests. To insure that this instrument is kept in optimum condition, we have a fundamental responsibility to eat properly. We owe it to ourselves to strive for the highest degree of wellness attainable. To do this we must begin by following certain basic rules for eating. The rules are simple. They are grounded in the inviolability of nature and have been verified by modern research. They are followed in all cultures where long life is the rule rather than the exception. They have been advocated by the healing traditions of ancient India, Greece and Persia and are being reemphasized today by many modern nutritional experts.

These general guidelines are listed below. If followed, they will assist the conscientious consumer in making the transition from excessive amounts of meat protein, fat and "empty calories" toward more nutritive high quality staples; away from refined foods toward whole, natural ones; away from a diet that fosters physical and emotional illness towards one that aids the individual in reaching his highest physical, mental and spiritual potential.

1

SELECTION

Freshness

The best foods are those which are the freshest and the least refined. By using fresh, unadulterated food, the nutritional value of food is maximized and the potential harm from the many artificial chemicals found in refining, processing and preserving is reduced. Each step in the refining process destroys the quality of the food, removing valuable nutrients. The longer fruits and vegetables sit on the grocery shelves, the more vitamins are destroyed.

Whole Grains

Use predominantly whole grains. Whole wheat or rye flour should be used instead of white flour whenever possible. When white flour is necessary, unbleached should be used. Eat brown or basmati rice instead of polished rice. Both white flour and polished rice have had their outer coating removed in the refining process. Since most of the vitamins, minerals and much of the protein value contained in this outer coating is lost, these products even after being "enriched" are nutritionally inferior to whole, unrefined grains.

Natural Sweeteners

Use natural sweeteners like honey,* sorghum, rice syrup, molasses and date sugar instead of white sugar. Sugar is a chemical, over 99% pure sucrose. This concentration can be found nowhere in nature. Over-consumption of sugar can lead to overweight and diabetes and may predispose one to the development of heart disease and ulcers to name a few of the whole assortment of illnesses associated with excessive

*Honey is best raw and unrefined, and should never be heated or used in cooking.

2

sugar intake. In general one should limit his sweet consumption. Substitution of these natural products, which are more slowly assimilated and hence less stressful to the body, is a good first step. It will be noted that some of the recipes in this book call for the use of sugar. Certainly for most of us, occasional use of sugar is acceptable. Rather than total abstention from sugar, discretion and moderation, as in all endeavors, seems to be the best policy.

Butter versus Margarine and Oil

Use butter and clarified butter for cooking rather than margarine or vegetable oil. In the early 60's the use of "polyunsaturated oils and margarine" was popularized. Interestingly, the main proponents of its use were the large food manufacturers. Based on some inconclusive evidence, it was felt that by using polyunsaturated oils rather than butter, one could lower the risk of developing a heart attack. More recently, however, research has shown that this may not be the case. In fact, scientific studies have now been performed that demonstrate the potential dangers of using these highly polyunsaturated oils, in that their use has been linked with the development of cancer and premature aging. Besides being a nutritious food, if not eaten in excess, butter possesses a marvelous flavor that is incomparable to margarine. Clarified butter is superb for cooking. It requires no refrigeration and is solid at room temperature, making it easy to use.

If one desires vegetable oils, then only fresh cold-pressed oils should be used. It is a combination of heating the oil to high temperatures during the extracting process and sitting on the shelf for long periods of time that produces the unhealthy properties alluded to above. Most commercial oils are prepared using high temperatures as well as using petroleum-like solvents to extract the oil. For this reason they should be avoided, and other sources—such as those obtainable at health food stores—should be sought.

3

PREPARATION

Food should be prepared with care. It should be well cleaned. Dirt and grit, if not removed, can harm the teeth. The tough and fibrous parts of fruits and vegetables are best removed by scrubbing with a stiff brush or peeling with a knife. Peel and rinds contain not only nutrients, but also indigestible, irritating roughage, potentially harmful natural chemicals, and—quite commonly—man-made insecticides.

Genuine home cooking is a means of self-expression. No restaurant cuisine, no matter how extravagant, can compare with a meal that has been patiently and carefully prepared at home. This is true simply because in the restaurant, the love and caring that goes into home cooking does not exist. By approaching cooking as an act of expressive creativity rather than as a routine chore, the quality of the meal will improve and one will gain a tremendous sense of satisfaction.

EATING

If food is prepared with loving attention, then it is the responsibility of those who eat the finished product to do so with an equal amount of consideration. Each mouthful should be chewed slowly and completely—about thirty-five times. There should be no external distraction during the meal such as television or a newspaper. When one eats, his consciousness should be focused upon his mouth and stomach, not back at work. It is best if one relaxes a few minutes before eating, allowing himself to let go of any tension so that the meal can be properly enjoyed and digested. Don't overeat. There is an old Chinese expression that says, "The first half of the meal is for the stomach and the second half for the doctor." By conscientiously following these simple rules, certain physiological and psychological changes will occur. First one's enjoyment and appreciation of food will improve. One will begin relishing the goodness and flavor of whole, natural foods and will lose the desire for rich spicy dishes, candy, soft drinks, and other non-nutritive "junk food." One will tend to eat less when essential nutrients are being supplied through good quality food. One's appetite will diminish and pounds of unwanted fat will melt away. Finally, one's overall physical health and emotional outlook will improve. Proper food preparation and eating are the foundations upon which well-being rests. We hope that these suggestions and the recipes that follow will help you along the road to good health—the yoga way.

Lawrence M. Cohen, M.D.

Basics

How to Make Clarified Butter

Place one pound of unsalted butter in a saucepan and heat until it boils. Lower heat and allow foam to accumulate on top. When the foam begins to thicken, skim it off, being careful not to stir up the butter. Be careful that the butter and the solids which adhere to the bottom of the pan do not burn. When the foamy milk solids are all skimmed off and a clear liquid remains in the pan, turn off the heat. Let the butter rest for a few minutes and then carefully pour it into a metal or earthenware vessel. Since clarified butter will last for weeks without refrigeration, keep it near your stove for ease in cooking. The skimmings can be added to vegetables for flavor.

How to Make Cheese

Pour a half gallon of milk into a pan and bring to a boil. Add the juice of two lemons to the center of the milk. Stir gently and allow to boil another few seconds. When milk has curdled, strain through cheesecloth or muslin and squeeze out the liquid until the desired consistency. If most of the liquid is squeezed out, the cheese can be refrigerated and later cut into squares for cooking. If some liquid is left in, the cheese will be soft like cottage cheese or cream cheese and can be spread. In its softened stage, it can also be whipped in a blender with a little milk and honey to make a delicious topping for fruit or cake. The liquid which separated from the cheese is whey and is quite healthful for the urinary system if a glass is drunk occasionally. Yields about one cup cheese and six cups whey.

How to Make Yogurt

Pour one quart of milk into a pan and bring to a boil. Let cool to 105-110° and add yogurt culture. Culture can be a few tablespoons of yogurt from a sugar-free prepared product, from a leftover batch of yogurt, or from a powdered package available at the health food store. Bulgarian starter is the best. Stir milk to dissolve the starter and pour into a quart jar. Cover jar with a dish towel and place in a warm place for about 4 to 5 hours. When yogurt has thickened and slips from the sides of the jar, place in refrigerator to gel. The amount of time yogurt rests in the warm spot as well as the moment the yogurt is refrigerated will affect the taste. Experiment with the timing yourself so that the yogurt will be as tart or as mild as you wish.

How to Make Sprouts

Put about one-fourth cup of beans or grains into a quart mason jar. (Alfalfa, mung, lentils, chick peas, wheat, etc. can all be sprouted.) Fill with water one inch above the beans. Soak beans overnight in a dark place. The next day, cover top of jar with cheesecloth held in place with a rubber band. Pour out water and rinse beans thoroughly every five or six hours with cool water. Rinsing can be done with cheesecloth in place. Continue this process for about three

7

days or until sprouts are the desired size. Sprouts can be "greened" in the sun for a few hours, if desired. Store sprouts in refrigerator like any green, leafy vegetable.

How to Make Tofu

Cover one cup of soy beans with three cups of water and soak for ten hours.

Boil five cups of water in a four-quart pot. Meanwhile blend half of the drained beans with one and one-half cups of water and add to the boiling water. Then blend the other half of the beans in the same way and add to the pot. Bring again to a boil and simmer for ten minutes, watching to prevent it from boiling over, and stirring constantly.

Strain the soybean mixture through a moist cheesecloth, double thickness, carefully collecting the liquid. Put the pulp remaining in the cheesecloth into the smaller pot filled with three cups of boiling water. Simmer the pulp for five minutes, stirring occasionally, and again strain through cheesecloth, collecting the liquid. Wearing rubber gloves to protect yourself from the heat, squeeze out all the soy milk from the cheesecloth by applying body force as you press the cheesecloth "sack" with a round, flat-bottomed steel bowl against the side of a larger bowl. Discard pulp.

Combine both batches of soy milk and bring it all to a boil. Remove from heat and thoroughly dissolve one teaspoon epsom salts or commercially prepared nigari in one cup of boiling water. (Keep this solution covered to retain heat.) Stir soy milk briskly with a circular motion. Reverse the direction and add half of the nigari solution. Stop stirring and watch for curdling; if none, add one to three teaspoons more nigari solution. Cover soy curds, let stand three minutes; then if whey is clear, proceed to next paragraph. If it is still cloudy, pour remaining nigari solution over inverted spoon held over the center and around the edge of the pot; then gently stir around the edge. Let sit for three minutes.

Line a pressing box with moist cheesecloth and gently

8

pour tofu (soy curds) through the cloth. Put the top on the box and press with a weight (a filled water jug will do or two or three bricks). When tofu reaches the desired consistency (about twenty minutes) gently remove it from the box and the cheesecloth and store it, covered, in a bowl filled with cold water. Tofu is best used within five days. Keep refrigerated and change the water daily. This recipe makes one pound of tofu. If the recipe is doubled the yield will fill the commercially available pressing boxes (4 x 3½ x 8 inches).

Special Ingredients

Arrowroot A thickening agent available in powdered form or chunks (1½ tablespoons of arrowroot to 1 cup of water).

Basmati rice Natural white rice grown in India around the city of Dehra-Dun. Available in Indian food stores.

Bok choy Chinese celery; available in Oriental food stores or in better produce stores.

Brewer's yeast A highly nutritious yeast by-product abundant in B vitamins; available in health food stores.

Brown rice Highly nutritious, unprocessed rice available in short or long grains.

Bulgur Parboiled cracked wheat; available in Middle Eastern or health food stores.

Carob Chocolate substitute made from carob pods; also known as St. John's bread. Available in powdered form and in chips.

Coriander leaves Fresh condiment available in Spanish or Indian food stores.

Date sugar Ground dates used as a sugar substitute. Available in health food stores.

Fructose Natural sugar derived from fruit; available in

health food stores.

Kefir   Cultured milk similar to yogurt. Also available in cheese form in dairy and health food stores.

Lecithin   Lineoleic and lineolinic acid processed from soybeans. Sold in granular form in health food stores.

Mung sprouts   Sprouted mung beans. Sold in produce stores, but better if homemade from mung beans (see recipe on page 7).

Raw sugar   Partially processed sugar, still containing some of the nutrients; available in health food stores.

Rice flour   Flour made from rice; available in Oriental and health food stores.

Rice syrup   Thick, sweet syrup made from rice and barley, used as a sugar substitute; available in health food stores.

Rose hips   Fruit of the rose plant, very high in vitamin C; available in health food stores.

Sesame butter   Ground sesame seeds, also called tahini; available in health food stores.

Sorghum   Heavy, sweet syrup made from sorghum cane, used as a sugar substitute.

Soy beans   Nutritious staple available whole, in granules, as flour, as grits (cracked, partially-boiled) and as miso (fermented soybean paste).

Tamari sauce   Condiment made from soy sauce.

Tofu   Soy bean curd; available at Japanese, Korean or health food stores. For homemade tofu see recipe on page 8.

Main
Dishes

MUSHROOM QUICHE

1 cup mushrooms, sliced
1 scallion, sliced
3 eggs
1 cup cream
1 cup yogurt
1 tablespoon minced fresh parsley
¼ teaspoon salt
1/8 teaspoon white pepper
1/8 teaspoon ground coriander
½ cup shredded swiss or cheddar cheese
¼ cup ground cashews
2 tablespoons wheat germ

Saute mushrooms and scallion. Beat eggs and add cream and yogurt; combine with the sauteed vegetables. Stir in parsley and seasonings. Add the cheese and cashews.

Generously butter a pie pan and sprinkle wheat germ evenly over it. Pour the custard mixture into it and bake for 35 to 40 minutes at 375° or until the top is golden brown. Serves 4 to 6.

Variation:

Two cups of warm, scalded milk and one large chopped onion may be substituted for the cream, yogurt and scallion. Cashews may be omitted.

GREEN QUICHE

Crust:
  1½ cups whole wheat flour
  3 tablespoons roasted sesame seeds, ground
  ½ teaspoon salt
  ¼ cup warm water
  ¼ cup clarified butter

Combine dry ingredients. Combine water and butter. Mix together, adding more water if necessary, to form a firm, but slightly moist dough. Roll out to fit a 9 inch pie pan. Prick with a fork and bake at 400° for about 10 minutes. Remove from oven and set aside.

Filling:
  2 onions, finely diced
  ¼ cup clarified butter
  1 pound spinach, cleaned and chopped
  1 cup yogurt
  1½ cups milk
  1 teaspoon salt
  1½ teaspoon tamari or soy sauce
  pinch black pepper
  2 teaspoons minced chives
  3 eggs, beaten
  ¼ pound ground cheddar cheese

Saute onion in butter until transparent. Add spinach, cover pan and steam until spinach is limp. Put spinach mixture in blender along with the remaining ingredients, excluding the cheese. Blend until smooth and creamy.

Sprinkle the grated cheese into the partially baked pie crust. Pour the quiche mixture over the cheese and bake at 400° for 40-60 minutes. Serves 4 to 6.

SPINACH QUICHE

8 inch whole wheat pastry shell (recipe pp. 16 or 18)
5 tablespoons butter
2 cups chopped fresh spinach, well packed
¾ teaspoon salt
¼ teaspoon pepper
½ teaspoon nutmeg
2 tablespoons finely minced green onions
3 eggs
½ cup cream
1½ cups grated swiss cheese

Partially bake pie shell at 400° until it starts to color and shrink from sides (approximately 10 minutes). Melt 1½ tablespoons butter in skillet; stir in chopped spinach, ¼ teaspoon salt, and pinches of pepper and nutmeg. Cover and cook very slowly for 2 minutes until spinach has released its juices. Uncover. Raise heat, stir for 2 to 3 minutes until all moisture has evaporated. Set aside.

Cook onions in 2 tablespoons butter. Add spinach and stir over moderate heat for several minutes. Remove from heat and stir in ¼ teaspoon salt, 1/8 teaspoon pepper, and the rest of the nutmeg. Beat eggs and cream with fork and add to spinach mixture. Pour into pie shell. Sprinkle with cheese, dot with remaining butter and bake 25 to 30 minutes in a 375° oven. Serves 4 to 6.

TOFU SPINACH PIE

Crust:
    1 cup whole wheat flour
    ¼ cup soy flour
    ½ teaspoon salt
    1/3 cup clarified butter, with enough water added
        to make ½ cup

Stir flours and salt together. Pour in butter and water and mix with a fork to form a ball. Roll out into a 9-inch circle between layers of waxed paper. Place in pie pan and set aside.

Filling:
    3/8 cup clarified butter
    4 small onions, chopped
    ½ teaspoon turmeric
    1 teaspoon ground cumin
    1 teaspoon ground coriander
    1¼ cups cooked spinach, chopped
    ¼ cup fresh parsley, chopped and packed
    ¼ cup fresh dill weed (or 1 tablespoon dried)
    1 teaspoon Spike seasoning
    1 teaspoon vegetable salt
    1 pound tofu

Saute onions and spices in clarified butter until onions are translucent and spices are brown. Stir in spinach, parsley, dill and seasonings. Crumble tofu with fingers into mixture. Combine well and pour into pie crust. Bake for 1 hour at 350°. Serves 5-6.

HIMALAYAN QUICHE

2½ cups milk
4 eggs
2 teaspoons salt
dash pepper
1½ teaspoons paprika
1 teaspoon summer savory
1 teaspoon basil
2 cups cooked basmati (natural white) rice
¼ cup ground sesame seeds
3 tablespoons clarified butter
¼ teaspoon turmeric
½ teaspoon cumin
¾ teaspoon coriander
2 medium onions, sliced into rings
½ pound mushrooms, sliced
2 yams, finely diced

Blend the first seven ingredients together and set aside.

Mix cooked rice and sesame seeds and press into a 9-inch pie pan.

Saute turmeric, cumin and coriander in the butter until brown. Add onions and fry until well browned. Add mushrooms and cook until brown. Then add yams and cook until soft. Spread vegetable mixture over the rice crust. Pour the milk mixture over the top. Bake at 400° for 40-60 minutes, until firm. Serve hot or cold. Serves 4-6.

VEGETABLE QUICHE

8 or 9-inch pie crust (recipe pp. 16 or 18)
½ cup finely sliced mushrooms
3 green onions, sliced
½ cup chopped broccoli
2 level tablespoons flour
½ teaspoon salt
sprinkle of nutmeg
sprinkle of freshly ground black pepper
1¾ cups milk
4 eggs, beaten
1 cup cubed cheese (muenster, monterey jack, gruyere
   or mozzarella)

Clean and chop vegetables and preheat the oven to 350°. Mix the dry ingredients with a little of the milk until smooth. Gradually add the rest of the milk and the beaten eggs. Put the vegetables and the cubed cheese into the pie crust and pour the quiche mixture over them to cover. Bake for 45 minutes until lightly browned. Serves 4-6.

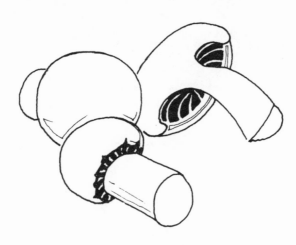

WHOLE WHEAT CHEESE BLINTZES

1 pound cottage cheese or pot cheese
3 eggs
½ teaspoon raw sugar
¾ teaspoon salt
dash of pepper
2/3 cup cold water
½ cup milk
1 cup whole wheat flour
2 tablespoons clarified butter
¼ cup butter
sour cream or applesauce

In a large bowl, mix together cheese, 1 of the eggs, sugar, ½ teaspoon of the salt, and pepper. Set aside.

Combine water, milk, remaining 2 eggs and remaining ¼ teaspoon salt in blender. Add flour and clarified butter; whirl at high speed for 1 minute. Scrape down sides of bowl with rubber spatula. Blend 30 seconds longer. (Batter should be the consistency of heavy cream. If too thick, add water.) Pour scant ¼ cup batter into lightly greased, hot 6 to 8-inch skillet, tilting pan quickly to cover bottom. Pour off excess batter. Cook over medium heat 1 minute or until bottom is golden. Turn out on waxed paper. Repeat with the remaining batter.

To fill blintzes, place 2 tablespoons cheese mixture at one edge of the cooked side. Fold in sides, envelope fashion, and roll up from the filled end. Brown in butter and serve hot with sour cream or applesauce. Serves 4.

CHEESE SOUFFLE ROLL-UP

Souffle:
> 7 eggs, separated
> 1/3 cup clarified butter
> dash cayenne pepper
> ¼ teaspoon cardamom
> 6 tablespoons unbleached flour
> ¾ teaspoon salt
> 1¼ cups milk
> ½ cup + 2 tablespoons grated parmesan cheese
> ½ cup coarsely grated cheddar or gruyere cheese
> 1 tablespoon wheat germ
> ¼ teaspoon cream of tartar

Filling:
> 1½ pounds fresh spinach, washed and cut
> ½ pound fresh kale, washed and cut
> 2 tablespoons clarified butter
> 2 teaspoons black mustard seed
> ¼ teaspoon cinnamon
> ½ cup chopped onions
> ¼ teaspoon salt
> ¼ cup cheddar cheese
> ¼ cup homemade cheese (recipe p. 6)
> ½ cup sour cream or kefir cheese
> about ¼ pound cheese slices (cheddar or gruyere)

Let eggs reach room temperature. Grease a 15 x 10 inch jelly roll pan, line the bottom with waxed paper and then grease paper with butter. Heat oven to 350º.

Prepare Souffle:
In saucepan, heat clarified butter. Add cardamom and cayenne and fry for about 1 minute. Remove from heat. With wire whisk, stir in flour and salt. Gradually add milk, return to heat, and stirring constantly, bring to a boil. Reduce

22

heat and continue to cook and to stir until mixture is smooth, thick, and leaves the bottom of the pan. Beat in ½ cup cheddar and ½ cup parmesan cheese. With whisk, beat egg yolks and add cheese mixture to it. In a separate bowl, beat the egg whites and cream of tartar until stiff. Fold egg whites into cheese mixture to combine. Turn mixture into the jelly roll pan and bake for 15 minutes or until surface is puffed up and firm. Remove from oven to cool.

Prepare Filling:

Cook spinach and kale in small amount of water. Drain well and squeeze out excess water. In a saucepan, heat butter until hot and add mustard seed. Fry until the seeds begin to pop. Add cinnamon and onion and fry until onion is translucent. Add the spinach-kale mixture, salt, cheeses and sour cream. Mix well. Remove from heat.

Loosen the cheese souffle from the pan and invert it on waxed paper that has been sprinkled with parmesan cheese and wheat germ. Peel off waxed paper from the other side. Spread the surface of the souffle with the spinach mixture. Roll up from the long side and place seam side down on a buttered cookie sheet. Arrange cheese slices on top and place in broiler, about 4 inches from heat, until cheese melts. Serve in generous slices. Serves 6.

BAKED NUT LOAF

½ cup raw cashews
½ cup raw almonds
½ cup walnuts
½ cup pecans
2/3 cup sunflower seeds
2/3 cup pumpkin seeds
2/3 cup sesame seeds
2 eggs
2 onions, quartered
½ cup cooked brown rice
¼ cup wheat germ
½ cup parsley, chopped
½ teaspoon sage
½ teaspoon thyme
½ teaspoon salt
½ teaspoon pepper
2 tablespoons brewer's yeast
1/3 teaspoon celery salt
1/3 cup grated cheddar cheese

In a blender, coarsely grind the nuts, half at a time. Put this meal in a small bowl and stir in the seeds. Put the eggs in a blender, drop in the onion and blend until smooth. Stir into the nut meal. Stir in the remaining ingredients except the cheese. Pat the mixture into a well-oiled cake plate. Bake at 350° for 25 minutes. Sprinkle with the grated cheese during the last 10 minutes of baking. Slice into wedges and serve, covered with Mushroom Cheese Sauce (recipe follows). Serves 6-8.

MUSHROOM CHEESE SAUCE

4 tablespoons butter
1 cup onions, finely chopped
2 cups mushrooms, sliced

¼ cup whole wheat flour
3 cups hot milk
1 teaspoon salt
¼ teaspoon black pepper
1½ cups kefir cheese or ricotta cheese, or half of each

Heat the butter in a 2 quart saucepan. Saute the onions and mushrooms until the onions are transparent.

Gradually stir in the flour, stirring constantly so that it coats the vegetables. Cook this mixture over gentle heat for about one minute, stirring all the time.

Add the milk, one cup at a time. Simmer the mixture until it has thickened slightly. Add the salt and pepper while mixture simmers.

Stir the cheese until it is separated and soft. Add cheese to the sauce and use a whisk to break up any lumps. The sauce is ready when it is hot.

VEGETARIAN CHOP SUEY

¼ cup clarified butter or oil
1 small onion, slivered
1 carrot, cut diagonally
½ green pepper, cut into strips
several stalks of bok choy, sliced
½ pound fresh mushrooms, sliced
½ cup sliced water chestnuts
2 cups fresh mung bean sprouts
2 small tomatoes, peeled
1 cup fresh snow pea pods
½ cup coarsely chopped walnuts
soy powder and tamari sauce as needed

Put clarified butter into a wok. When it gets hot, add onion and stir fry, turning constantly and quickly to cover with butter and cook evenly. Add carrot next and stir fry as for onion. Add each vegetable in turn in the order given. Then add the walnuts, stir, cover, and let steam for 3 to 5 minutes over low heat.

Pour off the liquid into a small pan; add soy powder and tamari sauce to taste and cook over low heat until thickened. Add this sauce to the vegetables and mix well. Cover again and heat about ten minutes to blend the flavors, adding water as needed until all ingredients are heated through, yet still slightly crisp.

Serve with rice. Makes about 4 servings.

VEGETARIAN CHILI

1 cup pinto beans
3 tablespoons butter
½ teaspoon turmeric
1 teaspoon ground cumin
1 teaspoon cumin seed
1 teaspoon ground coriander
1 large onion, chopped
3½ cups boiling water
½ teaspoon vegetable seasoning
1 teaspoon vegetable salt
1/8 teaspoon cayenne
½ teaspoon chili powder
½ pound mushrooms, chopped and sauteed
2 to 4 fresh tomatoes, peeled and cubed
1 green pepper, diced and simmered until soft

Pour boiling water over pinto beans and soak overnight. When ready to cook, melt butter in large pot and add
the first four spices. Let spices brown and then add onion,
drained beans, and boiling water. Cover partially and simmer
on lowest heat at least 3 hours until beans are soft enough
to mash between the fingers. Then add the last seven ingredients. Heat until all the flavors are well blended. Serve
with whole grain bread. Serves 8.

VEGETABLE PIZZA

Dough:
  1¼ cups whole wheat flour
  1½ cups unbleached flour
  ¾ cup milk
  1 package dry yeast
  ¼ cup warm water

Dissolve yeast in water. Mix flours together. Add yeast and milk and knead about 10-15 minutes. Cover and let rise about 1 hour. Punch down and divide in half. Spread half of the dough in a 9 x 13 inch pan to make a thin crust. (The other half is for a second pizza. Make now or later.) Spread melted butter over the crust. Keep covered until sauce is added so it will not dry out.

Sauce:
  3 tablespoons clarified butter
  2 carrots, chopped
  4 stalks of celery, chopped
  ½ green pepper
  ½ pound mushrooms
  2 tablespoons parsley
  1 tablespoon oregano
  1 teaspoon sweet basil
  ½ teaspoon dill weed
  a few green olives, chopped
  2 cups tomatoes, cooked down (or a 15 ounce can of
    tomato sauce)
  1 pound mozarella cheese, grated

Heat butter in a iron frying pan. Saute the carrots, celery, green pepper and mushrooms until soft. Add the spices and olives and cook until well blended. Remove vegetables from the frying pan and add to the tomato sauce and simmer, covered, for about 10 minutes. Spoon mixture

28

onto the crust, spreading to cover evenly. Bake at 350° for 25 minutes. Remove from oven, top with mozarella cheese, and bake for another 20 minutes until cheese is melted and brown. One pizza serves 4-6.

EGGPLANT PARMESAN

1 large eggplant
3 eggs, beaten
1 cup wheat germ
¾ cup clarified butter or oil
½ cup grated parmesan cheese
2 teaspoons oregano
½ pound mozzarella cheese, sliced
3 cups tomato sauce (recipe follows)

Start heating oven to 350°. Pare eggplant and cut into ¼ inch slices. Dip each slice in eggs, then in wheat germ. Saute eggplant in hot butter until golden brown. Place layer of eggplant in a 2 quart casserole; sprinkle with some of the parmesan, oregano and mozzarella. Then cover well with some of the tomato sauce. Repeat until all eggplant is used, topping last layer of sauce with a few slices of mozzarella. Bake for 30 minutes, or until sauce is bubbly and cheese is melted. Serves 4-6.

TOMATO SAUCE

4 large tomatoes, peeled and chopped
½ cup clarified butter or olive oil
1 cup finely chopped onion
1 clove garlic, crushed
6 ounces of tomato paste
2 sprigs parsley
1 tablespoon salt
2 teaspoons raw sugar
1 teaspoon oregano leaves
½ teaspoon dried basil leaves
¼ teaspoon pepper

Puree tomatoes in blender. In hot butter in a large

saucepan, saute onion and garlic until golden brown—about 5 minutes. Add pureed tomato, tomato paste, 1½ cups water, parsley sprigs, salt, sugar, oregano, basil and pepper. Mix well.

Bring to boil. Cover, reduce heat and simmer for 1 hour, stirring occasionally.

SOYBEAN TACOS

1 cup soybeans
5 cups water
1 tablespoon tamari sauce
1 teaspoon chili powder
1 teaspoon salt
½ teaspoon onion powder
dash of pepper
4 tablespoons butter

Measure the above ingredients into a pressure cooker. Mix well, cover and bring to 10 pounds of pressure. Cook for 30 minutes. Remove from heat and let the pressure reduce naturally.

¼ cup sunflower seeds
¼ cup sesame seeds
2 large onions, chopped
2 tablespoons chili powder
½ teaspoon black pepper
¼ cup clarified butter
4 large tomatoes
2 tablespoons fresh parsley, chopped
1 teaspoon fructose (optional)

Make sunflower and sesame meal by grinding the seeds in a blender, seed grinder, or coffee mill. Set aside.

Fry onions, chili powder and black pepper in butter until the onions become translucent and soft. Add the bean mixture, the meal from the seeds and mix well.Mash tomatoes and add to mixture. Add parsley and fructose and mix well. Simmer, uncovered, for 15 minutes or until mixture is almost dry.

Spoon mixture into a corn taco shell and add chopped

onions, shredded lettuce, shredded carrots, shredded cheese, chopped olives, finely chopped onions and finely chopped sweet banana peppers. This recipe fills 6-8 taco shells.

GARBANZO SPAGHETTI

1 - 1½ pounds whole wheat pasta noodles
2 tablespoons clarified butter or olive oil
1 garlic clove, minced
½ onion, chopped
2 medium carrots, chopped
1/3 cup chopped celery
1 green pepper, chopped
½ pound mushrooms, chopped
3 sprigs parsley, chopped
1 teaspoon sweet basil
1 teaspoon salt
dash of dill weed
½ teaspoon oregano
1 cup cooked garbanzo beans
2 cups tomatoes, cooked down
freshly grated parmesan cheese

Boil pasta in water until desired consistency.

Saute garlic and onion in the butter. Add carrot, celery, green pepper and mushrooms. Stir well. Add spices and beans and mix well. Cook for a few minutes until spices are blended. Remove from heat and add tomato sauce and mix well.

Serve on top of whole wheat pasta with fresh grated parmesan cheese on top. Serves 4-6.

Variation:

Spinach noodles may be used instead of whole wheat noodles.

½ cup split green peas may be substituted for the garbanzo beans.

SURPRISEBURGERS

½ pound lentils (1¼ cups)
3 cups water
1 large onion, chopped
1 cup chopped carrots
3 cups whole wheat bread crumbs
1 egg
1 teaspoon garlic salt
½ teaspoon crumbled oregano leaves
½ teaspoon salt
3 tablespoons butter
4 slices cheddar cheese, each slice cut into four
    triangles

Wash lentils; add water and bring to a boil in large saucepan. Lower heat; cover. Cook for 15 minutes.

Add onion and carrots. Cook 15 minutes more or until lentils are very tender. Remove from heat. Cool slightly. Stir in bread crumbs, egg, garlic salt, oregano and salt.

Melt butter in large skillet. Drop lentil mixture by rounded one-half cupfuls into hot butter. Flatten mounds into patties with pancake turner or broad spatula. Cook patties until firm and golden brown on both sides.

Top each patty with 2 cheese triangles; heat until melted. Garnish with parsley sprigs and carrot curls, if you wish. Makes 8 patties.

SOY BURGERS

2 cups soybeans
2 cups water
1 tablespoon baking soda
4 tablespoons clarified butter
1 teaspoon turmeric
2 teaspoons ground cumin
3 teaspoons ground coriander
2 onions, diced
1 green pepper, diced
½ cup whole wheat flour
½ cup dry bread crumbs
1 egg, beaten
2 teaspoons salt

Soak soybeans in water to which soda has been added. Pressure cook soybeans until tender (about 30 minutes at 10 pounds of pressure).

Put clarified butter in frying pan and heat until it bubbles; add turmeric, cumin and coriander. Fry until the spices begin to sizzle. Add onions and green pepper. Fry about 15 minutes or until the vegetables are very soft. Mash the soybeans with a potato masher and add flour, bread crumbs, egg and salt. Stir until well mixed and then add the onion-green pepper mixture. Shape into patties and fry until brown. Serve with tomato chutney (recipe p. 240).   Makes 8-10 burgers.

MILLET PATTIES

1 cup millet
4 cups boiling water
½ cup nut butter or ½ cup sunflower seeds
1 tablespoon clarified butter or oil
1 tablespoon soy sauce
2 tablespoons onion powder
1 teaspoon vegetable salt
celery seed, rosemary and thyme to taste

Cook millet by gradually adding it to boiling water, stirring constantly. Cover and cook on low heat for about 30 minutes or until the water is absorbed.

Add remaining ingredients. Form into patties and brown in a lightly buttered frying pan. Makes 8 patties.

POTATO PANCAKES
(Latkes)

6 large white potatoes
1 onion
2 eggs, slightly beaten
3 tablespoons whole wheat flour
1 teaspoon salt
¼ teaspoon pepper
about ¼ cup clarified butter or oil

Grate potatoes and onions. Stir in eggs. Add other ingredients, combining well. Drop by the rounded tablespoonful into hot butter, forming into a cake. Fry until crisp on both sides.

Serve hot with sour cream or applesauce and a crisp green salad. Makes 12-18 pancakes.

CARROT BURGERS

4 cups whole wheat bread crumbs
½ cup chopped walnuts
2 cups grated carrots
4 tablespoons grated onion
½ teaspoon salt
1/8 teaspoon pepper
3 eggs, beaten
¼ cup plus 1 tablespoon milk
clarified butter
a few slices of cheese (cheddar, mozzarella)

Combine all ingredients. Form into patties and fry in clarified butter in an iron frypan until brown on both sides. Place a slice of cheese on each patty and heat until cheese begins to melt. Makes about 8 patties.

TOFU BURGERS

¼ cup clarified butter
½ medium-size green bell pepper, chopped
4 to 5 medium-size mushrooms, chopped
1 small onion, chopped
¾ cup crumbled tofu
1½ cups cooked brown rice
1 egg, beaten
1½ tablespoons tamari or soy sauce
pinch of sweet basil
pinch of oregano
dash of salt
¼ cup whole wheat bread crumbs
½ cup whole wheat flour
1 teaspoon brewer's yeast

Saute chopped vegetables in butter until brown. Combine tofu and brown rice with fork. Add egg and mix well. Add tamari and spices and mix again. Then add bread crumbs, flour and yeast and mix well. Stir in cooked vegetables and let stand for a few minutes to allow the flavors to blend.

Shape into patties and fry in a small amount of clarified butter over medium-high heat until browned. Then turn and fry on the other side. Serves 8.

MILLET SOUFFLE

2 to 3 cups cooked millet
½ teaspoon salt
black pepper
½ cup or more grated cheese
2/3 cup milk
3 egg yolks
½ pound mushrooms, sliced   and stir-fried in 2 table-
    spoons of butter
3 egg whites

Combine all ingredients except egg whites.

Beat the egg whites until they form stiff peaks. Fold them very gently into the millet mixture, trying to maintain their volume. Don't worry if a few streaks of white remain.

Pour the mixture into a buttered 1½ quart baking dish. Bake at 350° for 30 to 45 minutes or until the center is firm. Serves 4 to 6.

MUSHROOM STROGANOFF

1 pound mushrooms, cleaned
1 small onion, diced
3 tablespoons butter
pinch of salt
pepper to taste
¼ cup lemon juice
2 tablespoons butter
2 tablespoons unbleached flour
1 cup sour cream
1 tablespoon minced chives or scallions

Cut large mushrooms in half. Saute mushrooms and onion in 3 tablespoons butter for about 5 minutes. Add seasoning and lemon juice and simmer over low heat. In a small frying pan, make a roux by melting 2 tablespoons butter and adding 2 tablespoons flour, stirring constantly. Add excess liquid from the mushrooms and cook, stirring constantly, until thickened. Add roux to mushrooms. Stir in sour cream and chives. Serve hot, over buttered whole wheat noodles. Serves 4.

BROCCOLI GARBANZO CASSEROLE

3 cups chopped broccoli
½ cup chopped onion
2 cups cooked brown rice
1 cup chopped mushrooms
1 cup cooked garbanzo beans
¾ cup grated sharp cheddar cheese
6 eggs
½ cup milk
1 teaspoon salt
¼ teaspoon pepper
1/8 teaspoon ground cardamom

Steam broccoli and onions. In a large bowl, combine broccoli, onions, rice, mushrooms, garbanzos, and half of the cheese. In another bowl, beat milk, eggs and seasonings. Pour egg mixture into the vegetables and mix well.

Pour mixture into a greased, shallow 2 quart casserole. Bake at 375° for 20 minutes. Sprinkle with the rest of the cheese and return to the oven for about 3 more minutes. Serves 4-6.

SPINACH NOODLE CASSEROLE

¾ pound spinach noodles
5 green onions, chopped
1 cup chopped mushrooms
¼ cup butter
5 large tomatoes, peeled and chopped
¼ cup chopped parsley
1 teaspoon sweet basil
dash oregano
dash thyme
dash rosemary
dash garlic salt
1 pint cottage cheese
1 teaspoon salt
¼ teaspoon pepper
3 ounces gruyere cheese, grated

Cook and drain the noodles. Saute onions and mushrooms in butter. In a large casserole, mix the noodles, onions, mushrooms, tomatoes, parsley and spices. Fold in the cottage cheese. Season to taste with the salt and pepper. Top with the grated cheese. Bake at 350° until bubbly. Serves 4-6.

GREEK SKILLET

1/3 cup clarified butter or olive oil
3 cups zucchini, cut into ¾ inch slices
3 cups eggplant, cut in ¾ inch slices
½ cup chopped onion
4 tomatoes, peeled and chopped
2 tablespoons chopped fresh mint, or 2 teaspoons
  dried mint
2 tablespoons chopped fresh dill, or 2 teaspoons
  dried dill
½ teaspoon salt
½ teaspoon pepper
½ cup yogurt
¾ pound feta cheese, crumbled

In a large skillet, heat butter. Saute zucchini, eggplant and onion for 5 minutes, stirring occasionally. Add tomatoes, mint, dill, salt and pepper. Cover and cook for 15 minutes. Stir in yogurt and heat an additional 3 minutes.

Just before serving, crumble feta cheese on top of the vegetables, sprinkling with additional mint. Serves 6.

KHORESHTE BADEJAN

1½ cups yellow split peas
1/8 to ¼ teaspoon cayenne
1/8 teaspoon ground cinnamon
1/8 teaspoon ground coriander
½ teaspoon turmeric
½ teaspoon ground cloves
½ teaspoon black pepper
pinch of salt
1 large onion, chopped
¼ pound mushrooms, chopped
2 large potatoes, diced
4 tablespoons clarified butter
2 apples, peeled and chopped

Cook the split peas until almost soft (about 1 hour). Saute the spices, onion, mushrooms, diced potatoes and apples in the butter, adding one ingredient at a time and stirring well after each is added. Then mix all ingredients together and put in a covered casserole. Bake at 350° for 45 minutes to 1 hour or until done. Serve with rice, millet or whole wheat bread. Serves 6-8.

TOFU RICE WITH VEGETABLES

clarified butter
½ teaspoon turmeric
2 teaspoons ground cumin
3 teaspoons ground coriander
2 onions, chopped
½ cup sliced mushrooms
2 tomatoes, peeled and chopped
¼ cup finely chopped celery
¼ cup finely chopped carrot
½ cup fresh peas or thawed frozen peas
2 teaspoons salt
1 teaspoon pepper
½ cup crumbled tofu
2 cups basmati (natural white) rice or brown rice
4 cups hot water

Preheat oven to 450°.

In a cast iron frying pan use clarified butter to fry turmeric, cumin and coriander. When spices start to turn dark, add chopped onion and stir well. Fry until the onions are translucent. Add sliced mushrooms and fry until they are soft. Add tomato and celery and carrot and cook until all the vegetables are soft, adding hot water when necessary to prevent sticking. Add the salt and pepper. Peas and tofu are added last and are just warmed.

Mix the rinsed rice into the vegetables and pour this mixture into a deep casserole, add 4 cups hot water, and cover. Bake for 1 hour. There is no need to stir. When all the water is gone and the rice is soft, the dish is ready to serve. Serves 8-12.

CARROT RICE LOAF

4 cups grated carrots
4 cups cooked brown rice
1 cup peanut butter, diluted with a little milk
½ cup raisins or currants
1 cup whole wheat bread crumbs
1 small onion, chopped
3 tablespoons minced parsley
1 tablespoon butter
pinch of salt
dash of pepper

Saute onion in butter. Combine onion with other ingredients and pour into a buttered loaf pan. Bake at 350° for 45 to 50 minutes. Serves 6.

Variation:
A combination of sesame butter and cashew butter may be substituted for the peanut butter.

SOYBEAN RICE

2 cups soybeans
1 cup basmati (natural white) or brown rice
½ cup shredded carrots
½ cup shredded fresh green beans
2¼ cups water
2 onions, finely chopped
1 green pepper, cut into strips
½ pound mushrooms, sliced
1 clove garlic, minced
3 tablespoons clarified butter
salt and pepper to taste

Soak the soybeans overnight; drain, rinse, and cover with water. Cook for 3 to 4 hours until tender. (If using a pressure cooker, cook for about 1 hour.) Drain beans and discard any loose skins.

Wash rice and add carrots and shredded green beans. Add water and bring to boil. Reduce to low flame and steam, covered, until all water is absorbed and rice stands on end. (If using brown rice, slightly more water will be required.)

In heavy skillet, saute onions, peppers, mushrooms and garlic in the butter. Season with salt and pepper. Toss these with the soybeans.

Place cooked rice in large casserole, pour the soybean mixture over the top and garnish with fresh parsley. Serves 6.

SCANDINAVIAN RICE-NUT LOAF

1 cup wheat germ
1½ cups cream or half milk and half cream
2 cups cooked rice
¼ cup melted butter
1 cup chopped or ground nuts
1 teaspoon salt
¼ teaspoon pepper
3 beaten eggs

Soak the wheat germ in the cream. Meanwhile, mix the rice, butter, nuts, salt, pepper and eggs together. Combine the two mixtures and pour into a buttered loaf pan.

Bake at 350° for about 1 hour. Cut into slices to serve. Serves 8.

Variation:

Kefir cheese or sour cream may be substituted for part of the cream in this recipe.

A variety of nuts can be used. Try pistachios, cashews and pine nuts as well as pecans and walnuts.

RISOTTO

1 cup split mung beans
2 cups uncooked rice
12 medium-size mushrooms
2 cloves garlic
1 small scallion, minced
2 tablespoons minced parsley
½ cup clarified butter
2 cups cooked tomatoes
about 5 cups hot vegetable broth
salt and pepper to taste
parmesan cheese, grated

Soak rice and beans in cold water for 30 minutes. Wash mushrooms and chop fine. Mash the garlic cloves and mix with minced fresh scallion and parsley.

In a saucepan heat clarified butter, put in garlic, scallion, parsley and mushrooms, and fry gently a few minutes. Add tomatoes, cover, and let simmer for 30 minutes.

Drain the rice and put into another saucepan with ½ cup broth. Cook, covered, until the broth has been absorbed. Then add another ½ cup of broth and so on, until the rice and beans are tender.

Stir in the tomato mixture, season to taste, and cook about 30 minutes longer. Sprinkle with cheese. Serves 8.

RICE VEGETARIAN DINNER

6 tablespoons butter
1 cup finely chopped green onions
1 cup sliced celery
1 cup finely chopped green pepper
6 mushrooms, chopped
4 cups cooked brown rice
¾ cup chopped almonds or walnuts
¼ cup raisins
½ cup vegetable stock or water
1 tomato, sliced
4 ounces cheddar cheese, thinly sliced

Melt butter; add onions, celery, green pepper and mushrooms and saute until soft. Add brown rice, nuts and raisins. Add vegetable stock until all ingredients are well moistened. Place tomato slices over top. Layer with cheese. Cover and cook for 5 to 10 minutes. Serves 4-6.

PIGNOLIA PILAF

2 large onions, chopped
4 tablespoons clarified butter
2 cups brown rice
¼ cup pignolia nuts, chopped
¼ cup green pepper, finely chopped
½ cup fresh green peas
¼ cup shredded carrots
¼ cup currants
2 tomatoes, peeled and chopped
4 cups vegetable stock
¼ teaspoon sage
1 tablespoon minced parsley
½ teaspoon allspice
¼ teaspoon cinnamon
vegetable salt to taste

Saute onions in butter until transparent. Stir in the rice and nuts and fry for about 5 minutes. Add remaining ingredients.

Cover with a tight-fitting lid and cook over a very low heat until all liquid is absorbed, about 45 minutes. Serves 8.

PARMESAN ZUCCHINI RICE

1 cup raw brown rice, cooked in 3 cups of water
and ½ teaspoon salt
2 tablespoons butter
½ cup grated parmesan cheese
juice of 1 lemon
¼ cup water
¼ teaspoon pepper
1 egg, beaten
3 medium zucchini, scraped and split lengthwise
grated parmesan cheese, as desired
1/3 cup hulled sesame seed
butter, as desired

Stir the butter into the hot, cooked rice. Mix the grated cheese, lemon juice, water and pepper into the beaten egg. Blend this into the rice. Put into a buttered baking dish. Spread the zucchini on top and sprinkle with additional grated parmesan cheese and the sesame seed. Dot with additional butter. Bake at 350°, covered, until the zucchini are done, about 45 minutes. Serves 6.

BARLEY PILAF

clarified butter
2 teaspoons black mustard seed
2 teaspoons cumin seed
2 medium onions, thinly sliced
½ pound mushrooms, thinly sliced
¾ cup homemade cheese, crumbled (recipe p. 6)
2 teaspoons salt
2 cups barley
4½ cups water

In a cast iron frying pan, fry black mustard seed and cumin seed in about 2 tablespoons of the clarified butter until they begin to crackle. Add onions and cook until they are soft and transparent. Add mushrooms and cook until tender. Then add cheese and cook until well coated with spices and quite soft. Remove from heat.

Rinse barley until clean. Add vegetable and spice mixture and salt to barley, mixing thoroughly. Put mixture in a medium-size casserole, covering with the water. Cover and bake in a 450° oven for about 1½ hours, or until dry. Serves 10.

DELICIOUS KNISHES

Pastry:
> 2 cups whole wheat flour
> ½ cup melted butter
> ½ teaspoon salt
> ¼ to ½ cup water, as needed

Make pastry by adding butter and salt to flour and then water to reach a stiff consistency. Knead for 5 to 10 minutes to develop gluten. Then form into 1½ inch balls. Roll out to circles about 6 inches in diameter.

Filling:
> ¼ cup chopped onion
> 1/3 cup chopped celery
> 20 medium mushrooms, chopped
> 2 tablespoons chopped vegetables (zucchini, carrots, broccoli, etc.)
> ½ cup cooked rice
> ½ cup cooked lentils
> ½ teaspoon salt
> ¼ teaspoon pepper
> 1 teaspoon chopped fresh dill
> 1/8 teaspoon sage

Saute vegetables in a little butter. Add rice, lentils and seasonings. Heat through to distribute flavors. Place 2 tablespoons of filling in the center of each pastry, fold over, pinch closed. Flatten knishes into hockey-puck shaped circles.

Bake at 375° for about 40 minutes, until dough is browned. Serve with a fresh, green salad. Serves 6.

BLACK-EYED PEAS WITH CORNMEAL DUMPLINGS

1 onion, chopped
4 tablespoons clarified butter
2 cups black-eyed peas
6 cups water
1 carrot, peeled and sliced thin
1 tablespoon chopped parsley
2 teaspoons salt
1 teaspoon black pepper
1 vegetable bouillon cube
1 teaspoon brewer's yeast

Brown onions in clarified butter in bottom of pressure cooker. Add remaining ingredients. Cook for 30 to 40 minutes. Reduce pressure instantly. Return to heat and add dumplings.

Dumplings:
½ cup whole wheat or rice flour
½ cup cornmeal
¼ cup milk or soy milk
2 teaspoons baking powder
1 teaspoon salt

Mix well and drop by tablespoons in boiling liquid. Cover tightly and simmer for 15 to 20 minutes. Serves 8.

CURRIED STUFFED TOMATOES

6 large, firm, ripe tomatoes, washed
5 tablespoons clarified butter
2 small onions, finely chopped
1 teaspoon ground turmeric
1 teaspoon chili powder
1/8 teaspoon ground ginger
2 teaspoons ground cumin
3 teaspoons ground coriander
1/8 teaspoon ground cardamom
1/8 teaspoon ground cinnamon
pinch of ground cloves
1 cup basmati (natural white) rice
1 cup strained tomato pulp (from hollowed-out
    tomatoes)
1¼ cups water
1 teaspoon salt
1 cup baby green peas, steamed

Slice off top quarter of each tomato, then hollow tomatoes out leaving shells about ¼ inch thick. Drain upside down on paper towels. Press tomato pulp through a sieve to extract juice. Measure out and reserve 1 cup of the juice.

Heat 3 tablespoons of the butter in a large, heavy saucepan. Add onions and stir-fry about 10 minutes until soft and lightly browned. Blend in all spices and let mellow over low heat about 5 minutes. Add rice and heat and stir about 5 minutes until glistening.

Add strained tomato pulp, water and 1 teaspoon salt and bring to a rapid boil. Adjust the heat so that the mixture bubbles gently and cook, uncovered, 10 minutes. Stir in peas; cover and cook about 10 minutes longer, until rice is tender and peas are cooked through. If all liquid has not been absorbed, turn heat to lowest point and cook, uncovered, for a few minutes.

Lightly salt the hollow of each tomato; place tomatoes

in a shallow baking pan and fill with the curried rice and pea mixture, spooning it in lightly and mounding it up on top; drizzle with the 2 remaining tablespoons of butter.

Bake, uncovered, in a moderate oven (350°) for about 15 minutes, or just until tomatoes are piping hot. Serves 6.

Variation:

1 cup of homemade cheese (recipe p. 6) can be added to the curried rice mixture just before baking.

Slices of cheddar cheese can be added to the top of the tomatoes during the last 5 minutes of baking.

Spoon yogurt over the top of each tomato when serving.

STUFFED BUTTERNUT SQUASH

3 medium-size butternut squash
1 cup brown rice
½ cup green lentils
4 green onions or 1 medium-size white onion
2 stalks celery, finely chopped
2 ripe tomatoes
4½ cups water
½ teaspoon turmeric
1 teaspoon ground cumin
1½ teaspoons ground coriander
½ teaspoon sage
¾ teaspoon thyme
2 teaspoons salt

Wash the squash and slice lengthwise. Remove seeds. Place upside down in pan of water and steam in hot oven until almost done. While squash is cooking, place rice, lentils and water in pressure cooker and cook under 15 pounds of pressure for 20-25 minutes. In a regular saucepan, cook about 1½ hours. Remove from heat and depressurize. Remove cover and continue cooking on top of the stove until the grain is dry.

Combine turmeric, cumin and coriander. Fry in hot pan until browned, about 1 minute. Add onions and cook until transparent. Add celery and tomatoes and cook until the celery is soft. Add sage, thyme and salt. Combine this with rice and beans. Use as a filling in the squash and bake in 350° oven for 20-30 minutes. The squash may be sprinkled with shredded cheese and topped with alfalfa sprouts before serving. Serves 6.

COCONUT RICE AND BEANS

meat of 1 fresh coconut, grated
water
1 cup red beans
1 sprig fresh thyme or 1 teaspoon dried thyme
2 slices hot pepper or ¼ teaspoon chili powder
1 clove garlic, crushed
1 stalk scallion, chopped
pinch of salt
dash of fresh ground pepper
1 pound washed rice (about 2½ - 3 cups)

Make 1¼ quarts of coconut milk by adding water to the grated coconut. Let stand for 15 minutes, stir well, and strain through sieve.

Clean red beans, wash, and add to milk. Boil until tender (about 1 hour).

Add thyme, hot pepper, garlic, scallion, salt and pepper to beans. Simmer for 2 minutes. Add washed rice (liquid should be about 1 inch above rice). Bring to a boil, cover, and cook over low heat until liquid disappears and rice is tender. Serve with plantain or bananas. Serves 4.

Variation:

Serve this recipe with fresh summer fruit, such as papaya, mangoes, pineapple and melons.

SOMETHING LIGHT

3 cups cooked rice
¼ cup finely chopped scallions
1½ cups cottage cheese or ricotta cheese
1 clove garlic, minced
1 cup sour cream or yogurt
¼ cup milk
dash tobasco
½ teaspoon salt
½ cup grated parmesan cheese

Combine ingredients in the order listed and pour into a greased 1½ quart casserole. Bake uncovered for 25 minutes in a 350° oven.

Serve with a crisp salad and something heavy (lentils, whole wheat bread, etc.) Serves 6.

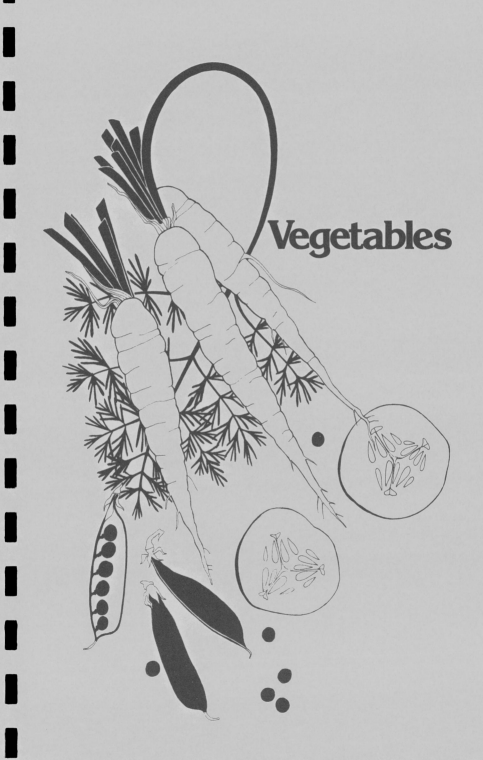

Vegetables

CREAMED BROCCOLI RING

2½ pounds broccoli, cleaned
4 eggs, beaten
1½ teaspoons salt
¼ cup heavy cream
¼ teaspoon ground pepper
¼ teaspoon ground nutmeg
2 teaspoons butter, softened
1 tablespoon wheat germ

Cook broccoli in boiling salted water in a large kettle or Dutch oven until tender, about 15 minutes. Drain and let cool. Chop into small pieces to fit an electric blender or food processor; puree.

Combine the broccoli puree, eggs, salt, heavy cream, pepper, nutmeg and wheat germ in a large bowl. Butter a 4-cup ring mold with the softened butter. Spoon the broccoli mixture into the mold and cover with foil.

Place mold in larger pan; pour in boiling water to a depth of 1 inch.

Bake in a moderate oven (350°) for 30 minutes or until custard is set. Unmold and serve with creamed onions (recipe p. 72), if desired. Serves 8.

BROCCOLI CASSEROLE

2 cups chopped onions
4 tablespoons butter
3 tablespoons flour
1 teaspoon salt
¼ teaspoon pepper
2 cups buttermilk
2 cups bread crumbs
1 cup cooked rice
1½ cups broccoli, chopped and steamed until just
    tender but still quite firm
6 slices cheese (cheddar or monterey jack)

Saute onions in half of the butter. Stir in flour, salt and pepper; cook until mixture bubbles. Stir in milk and cook on low heat until mixture thickens; boil for one minute.

Combine bread crumbs with the rest of the butter. Spread cooked rice in a buttered casserole. Cover with the cooked broccoli. Pour milk sauce over the broccoli and cover with slices of cheese. Top with bread crumbs.

Bake at 350° for 45 minutes. Serves 6.

MUSTARD BRUSSELS SPROUTS

10 to 16 ounces fresh brussels sprouts
½ cup water
½ teaspoon caraway seed
1/8 teaspoon cinnamon
½ teaspoon salt
¼ cup sour cream
1 tablespoon prepared mustard
dash of pepper

Bring sprouts, water, caraway seed, cinnamon and salt to boil; cover and simmer for 10 to 12 minutes or until crisp-tender. Drain well.

Combine sour cream, mustard and pepper and stir into brussels sprouts. Serve immediately. Serves 4.

CABBAGE SURPRISE

1 small head cabbage, shredded
1 medium-size onion, chopped
3 tablespoons clarified butter
1 cup sliced mushrooms
2 large apples, peeled and sliced
½ teaspoon salt
¼ teaspoon black pepper

In a large skillet, cook onion in butter until transparent. Stir in cabbage and mushrooms and fry for a few minutes. Add apples, salt and pepper. Stir-fry until ingredients are coated with butter.

Cover skillet and cook over medium heat for about 10 minutes, stirring occasionally. Serves 4-6.

CAULIFLOWER CRUNCH

3 cups diced cauliflower
½ cup hot water
2 tablespoons clarified butter
½ cup cubed cheddar cheese
2 tablespoons soy grits, soaked in 2 tablespoons
   water
¼ cup ground walnuts
3 tablespoons brewer's yeast
3 tablespoons soy powder
1 egg
½ cup toasted wheat germ
¼ cup rose hips
½ teaspoon sea salt
¼ teaspoon black pepper
¼ teaspoon nutmeg
½ cup ground cashews

Preheat oven to 350°. Blend cauliflower, water, butter and cheese thoroughly in blender. Combine with remaining ingredients, except cashews. Turn into a 2 quart casserole, top with cashews and bake for 35 to 45 minutes. Serves 6.

CHINESE CELERY

½ cup butter
1 large head bok choy (chinese celery), trimmed,
 washed and coarsely chopped
½ cup mung bean sprouts
½ cup fresh snow peas
½ cup shredded raw carrot
2 teaspoons tamari or soy sauce
¼ teaspoon salt
¼ teaspoon black pepper
pinch of ground cinnamon
pinch of ground ginger
½ cup wheat germ
¼ cup slivered almonds, toasted

In a large skillet, melt half of the butter over moderate heat; add celery and cook until the celery becomes slightly translucent. Add bean sprouts, peas, carrots and tamari and cook for another few minutes. Add the spices and mix well.

Transfer the mixture to a medium-size casserole and sprinkle with wheat germ. Dot with the remaining butter.

Bake at 350° for 40 minutes or until the top is crisp and brown. Remove from the oven and sprinkle with almonds. Serves 4.

ONION CASSEROLE

about 16 fresh green beans
6 medium-size onions
1 cup milk
1 cup mushrooms, finely chopped
1 tablespoon arrowroot
1 cup grated natural cheese
½ cup whole wheat bread crumbs

Steam green beans for a minute; remove to cutting board and dice very fine. Peel and dice onions very fine. Put beans and onions in a mixing bowl. Add milk, mushrooms, arrowroot and cheese; mix well. Pour into a buttered casserole. Top with whole wheat bread crumbs and bake at 350° for 1 hour, or until tender. Serves 4.

Variations:
Crumbled homemade cheese (recipe p. 6) may be substituted for the grated natural cheese.
Wheat germ may be substituted for, or combined with the bread crumbs.

CREAMED ONIONS

40 small white onions, peeled
1 tablespoon parsley, minced
6 tablespoons butter
6 tablespoons whole wheat or unbleached flour
1½ teaspoons salt
¼ teaspoon white pepper
¼ teaspoon ground nutmeg
3 cups milk
½ cup heavy cream

Cook onions, covered, in boiling salted water in a large saucepan until tender, about 15 minutes. Drain, reserving the cooking liquid.

Melt the butter in a large saucepan. Stir in the flour, salt, pepper, nutmeg and parsley and cook for 7 minutes. Remove pan from heat; stir in milk and heavy cream until smooth. Bring to boiling; lower heat; simmer about 5 minutes, stirring constantly, until sauce is thick and smooth. Add onions.

Note: If not serving at once, cover the surface of the creamed onions with a disc of lightly buttered waxed paper. Sauce may be thinned with reserved cooking liquid. Serves 8.

CURRIED NEW POTATOES

12 small, new potatoes of uniform size
2 large onions, chopped
1 clove garlic, crushed
2 teaspoons minced fresh ginger
6 tablespoons clarified butter
¼ teaspoon ground turmeric
½ teaspoon ground cumin
¾ teaspoon ground coriander
1/8 teaspoon ground cinnamon
¼ cup water
½ teaspoon salt

Place potatoes in a medium-size saucepan; cover with cold water, bring to boil; cover and boil for 20 minutes. Drain, cool and peel.

Stir-fry onions, garlic and ginger in 4 tablespoons of the butter in a large skillet until very soft and lightly browned. Mix in seasonings and heat for 2 to 3 minutes. Add the water and salt. Cover, turn heat to low and simmer for 15 minutes.

Heat remaining butter in a second large skillet just until bubbly; add potatoes and brown lightly. Transfer onion mixture to potatoes, spooning over all. Cover and cook for 5 minutes until the flavors are blended. Serves 4-6.

73

POTATO CASSEROLE

2 pounds potatoes, peeled and grated
salt
freshly ground black pepper
½ teaspoon nutmeg
1 egg, beaten
3 cups milk
¼ pound swiss cheese, grated
1 clove garlic, cut in half
3 tablespoons butter
grated cheese

Mix potatoes with salt, pepper, nutmeg, egg, milk and grated cheese. Butter a casserole and rub well with garlic pieces; spoon in the potato mixture. Sprinkle top lavishly with more cheese and dot with lumps of butter. Cook in medium-hot oven (375°) for 40 to 45 minutes. Serves 4-6.

Variation:
3 tablespoons of minced chives or parsley may be added along with the cheese.

CREAMED POTATOES

3 tablespoons butter
1 medium-size onion, chopped
1 green pepper, chopped
3 to 4 cups peeled, cubed raw potatoes
1 tablespoon chopped pimento
salt and pepper to taste
fresh parsley, chopped
½ cup dairy sour cream

In a skillet, saute onion in butter. Add green pepper, potatoes and pimento. Fry over high heat, turning often with a pancake turner. If potatoes brown before the other vegetables are done, cover and turn heat to low.

Serve topped with sour cream and fresh parsley. Serves 4-6.

Variation:
Try Kefir cheese in place of the sour cream to top the potatoes.

SCALLOPED POTATOES AND CARROTS

2 cups boiling water
2 teaspoons salt
2 pounds of potatoes, pared and thinly sliced (about
   5 cups)
1½ cups sliced onion
5 medium-size carrots, pared and sliced diagonally,
   ¼ inch thick
3 tablespoons butter
2 tablespoons whole wheat flour
1 teaspoon salt
¼ teaspoon pepper
dash cayenne
1½ cups milk
1½ cups grated sharp cheddar cheese
1 tablespoon minced parsley

Preheat oven to 375°. Lightly grease a 2½ quart baking dish.

In 2 cups boiling water in a large skillet, cook 2 teaspoons salt, potatoes, onions and carrots, covered, for 5 minutes or just until partially tender. Drain.

For cheese sauce, melt butter in a small saucepan; remove from heat; stir in flour, salt, pepper and cayenne; then stir in milk, blending well. Over medium heat, bring to a boil, stirring until smooth. Stir in 1 cup cheese. Cook until cheese is melted. Add parsley and stir.

In a casserole, layer half the potato, onion and carrot; top with half of the cheese sauce; repeat with other half of the vegetables and sauce. Sprinkle top with remaining cheese.

Bake, covered with foil for 30 minutes, or until potato is tender when pierced with a fork. If desired, uncover top during the last 10 minutes of baking to brown the top. Serves 6.

PEANUT-CARROTS

2 tablespoons clarified butter
1 teaspoon cumin seed
½ teaspoon mustard seed
2 cups carrots, peeled and grated
¼ cup roasted peanuts, broken into halves
salt
1 fresh lemon or lime
½ cup grated fresh coconut
¼ cup chopped fresh coriander leaves

Note: If using raw peanuts, roast in a 400° oven for about 15 minutes until brown. If using pre-roasted peanuts that are salted, adjust the salt in the recipe. Peanuts should have no skins. It is important that only very fresh peanuts are used.

Heat butter; add cumin seed and mustard seed. When the mustard seed begins to pop, add grated carrots and peanuts. Fry carrots for about 10 minutes or until almost cooked. Add salt to taste. Squeeze fresh lemon or lime over carrots. Cook another 5 to 10 minutes. When carrots are tender, sprinkle coconut and fresh coriander leaves over all. Be careful not to overcook the carrots; they should be tender, but not limp. Serves 4.

ZUCCHINI-CARROT PANCAKES

2 cups grated zucchini
1½ cups grated carrots
¾ cup unbleached flour
1 1/8 teaspoons baking powder
salt and pepper
1 egg, beaten
clarified butter
grated parmesan cheese

Combine zucchini, carrots, flour and baking powder; add salt and pepper to taste. Add the egg and stir to blend all the ingredients. Drop mixture by large tablespoons onto a hot griddle coated with clarified butter. Cook until brown on both sides. Sprinkle with grated cheese and serve. Makes about 12 pancakes.

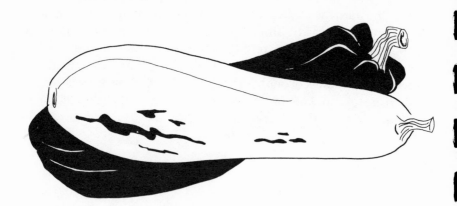

SPROUTED SOYBEANS

3 cups sprouted soybeans
¼ cup finely cut scallions
1 cup sliced mushrooms
½ cup shredded carrots
3 tablespoons clarified butter
1 tablespoon minced parsley
1 teaspoon herb seasoning
3 tablespoons tamari or soy sauce

In skillet, brown scallions, bean sprouts and mushrooms lightly in butter. Add carrot and parsley and stir. Add seasonings. Pour tamari over mixture and simmer for about 3 minutes. Serve with rice. Makes about 4 servings.

Note: See recipe on p. 7 for instructions for sprouting soybeans.

SPINACH CASSEROLE

1 onion, minced
¼ cup butter
3 tablespoons flour
2 cups milk
4 cups fresh, cooked spinach, drained
3 hard-cooked eggs, chopped
2 teaspoons salt
¼ teaspoon pepper
1/8 teaspoon nutmeg
2 cups wheat germ or whole wheat bread crumbs
½ cup grated cheddar cheese
2 tablespoons melted butter
paprika

Saute onions in ¼ cup butter until tender. Stir in flour. Add milk gradually, stirring until thickened. Add spinach, eggs and seasonings, mixing gently.

Place into a greased, shallow casserole. Mix wheat germ, cheese and butter and sprinkle over the top. Shake on paprika and bake in a 375° oven for 20 minutes. Serves 6.

Variation:
Add 1 cup of cooked rice, increasing milk to 2¼ cups.

SPINACH SOUFFLE WITH MORNAY SAUCE

1 cup cooked spinach
3 tablespoons butter
4 tablespoons whole wheat flour
1 cup light cream
6 egg yolks
pepper
pinch of nutmeg
7 egg whites
1 teaspoon salt, as desired
1/8 teaspoon cream of tartar

Preheat oven to 400°.

Place spinach in a blender; puree.

Melt butter; add flour and cream, stirring constantly to form a thick sauce. Remove from heat and add egg yolks one at a time. Add pepper to taste. Add a pinch of nutmeg.

Beat egg whites until stiff, adding salt and cream of tartar during beating. Combine spinach and sauce and fold in egg white gently. Pour into an oiled souffle mold or casserole.

Turn oven to 375° and bake souffle for 25 minutes.

Sauce:
1 tablespoon butter
1 tablespoon flour
1 cup cream
¾ cup grated cheese (parmesan or monterey jack)

Cream butter and flour over low heat. Add cream and grated cheese. Cook until thick and creamy.

Serve sauce over generous portions of the souffle. Serves 4.

81

SQUASH RING

3 cups mashed squash
¼ cup clarified butter
¼ cup milk
3 eggs, well beaten
½ cup grated onion
½ teaspoon sea salt or herb seasoning

Combine all ingredients; stir well. Pour into an oiled 5½ cup ring mold. Set in a pan of hot water and bake at 350° for 1 hour.

Unmold on a warm plate and fill the center with broccoli, Brussels sprouts, or other green vegetable of your choice. Serves 4-6.

SQUASH/APPLE/WALNUT PUREE

6 pounds winter squash, washed (preferably a combination of butternut, acorn and hubbard)
6 large baking apples, washed
6 tablespoons butter
1 teaspoon ground coriander
¼ teaspoon pepper
1 teaspoon salt, or more to taste
1 cup coarsely chopped walnuts
1 cup dry whole wheat bread crumbs
2 tablespoons frozen butter

Arrange the whole squash on a large pan or baking sheet and place in a cold oven. Turn oven on to 350° and bake squash until soft (45 minutes to 1½ hours).

Make a few holes in the apples with a skewer and place them in the baking pan with the squash about 45 minutes before you expect the last squash to be cooked through.

When both squash and apples are tender, remove them from the oven and cut each in half to cool. Scrape out the seeds of the squash and pull off the skins. Remove the skins and cores from the apples. Mix the squash and apples. Beat in the butter, coriander, pepper and salt.

Combine walnuts and bread crumbs. Spread the squash puree in buttered baking dishes. Sprinkle the nut-crumb mixture evenly over each dish. Shave the frozen butter over the top.

Bake in the top third of a preheated 425° oven for 30 minutes, until the puree is browned and bubbling. Serves 10-12.

HOLIDAY STUFFED SQUASH

2 buttercup or acorn squash, washed, cut in half,
  and with seeds removed
¼ cup maple syrup
¼ cup chopped pecans
1 large apple, peeled, cored and cubed
wheat germ
2 tablespoons butter
¼ teaspoon cinnamon (optional)

Combine maple syrup, pecans and apple. Put 1 tablespoon of this mixture into each of the squash halves, sprinkle
with wheat germ and cinnamon and dot with butter. Place
squash in a baking dish, cover, and bake at 350° for 1¼
hours or until tender. Serves 4.

SQUASH SOUFFLE

4 eggs, separated
2 cups squash, cooked and mashed
½ cup milk or cream
½ teaspoon herb seasoning
2 tablespoons arrowroot
1 cup grated natural cheese

Beat egg yolks with mixer; gradually add squash, milk, herb seasonings and arrowroot. Stir in grated cheese. Beat egg whites until stiff and fold into mixture. Pour into an oiled souffle mold or casserole and bake at 350° for 30 minutes. Serves 4.

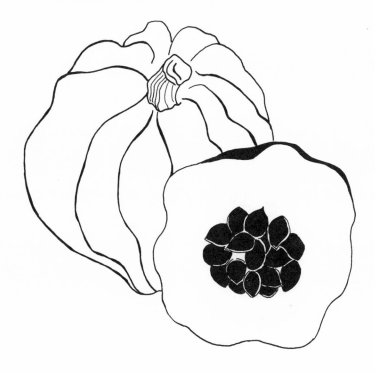

RICE STUFFED PEPPERS

5 medium-size green peppers
½ cup chopped onion
½ cup chopped celery
2 tablespoons clarified butter
pulp of 4 fresh tomatoes
1 teaspoon herb seasoning
2½ cups steamed brown or wild rice
grated parmesan cheese

Wash peppers and remove tops. Scrape out the seeds into a small bowl; set aside.

Saute onion and celery in butter; add tomato pulp, seeds from the peppers, herb seasoning and steamed rice. Fill peppers with this mixture, sprinkle with cheese, and bake in an oiled baking dish at 350° for 45 minutes or until tender. Serves 5.

TURNIPS AU GRATIN

1¼ cups milk
1 small clove garlic, peeled, with several cuts made
   in it
3/8 cup heavy cream
¼ stick (1/8 cup) butter
1½ tablespoons whole wheat flour
1/8 teaspoon nutmeg
¼ teaspoon dried thyme
1/8 teaspoon pepper
1/8 teaspoon dried, crumbled rosemary
½ teaspoon salt
2 pounds small white turnips, peeled, halved lengthwise, then cut across into slices ¼ inch thick (6 to
   7 cups)
¼ cup very fine whole wheat bread crumbs
1/3 cup grated parmesan cheese

Combine the milk, garlic and cream in a heavy saucepan and bring just to a simmer. Preheat the oven to 375°.
   Melt the butter in a skillet; stir in the flour and cook,
stirring, for 1 minute. Add the hot milk and stir with a whisk
over moderate heat until the mixture is thick and boiling.
Lower the heat and simmer for 5 minutes, stirring often.
Remove the garlic clove; add nutmeg, thyme, pepper, rosemary and salt. Remove from heat.
   While the sauce is cooking, bring a large pot of lightly
salted water to a boil. Drop in the sliced turnips and return
just to a boil over the highest heat. Drain well.
   Butter a 1½ - 2 quart baking dish. Arrange the turnips
in it. Pour the sauce over the turnips; cover with foil.
   Bake for 30 minutes. Remove the foil and sprinkle
casserole with the crumbs and then with the cheese. Turn
the oven to 425°. Continue to bake, uncovered, for 15 to
30 minutes, or until lightly browned and bubbling. Serves
8-10.

87

TEMPURA

2 egg yolks
1 cup water
1 cup unsifted whole wheat flour or chick pea flour
1 teaspoon salt
½ pound fresh mushrooms, sliced
½ pound small, whole green beans
2 sweet potatoes, thinly sliced
1 large sweet onion, cut in small wedges
1 small cauliflower, separated into flowerettes
1 bunch broccoli, flowerettes only
1 small zucchini, sliced
clarified butter or oil, in deep wok
1 cup vegetable broth
1/3 cup tamari sauce
1/3 cup lemon juice
grated ginger

Combine the eggs and water and beat until frothy. Add the flour and salt. Blend.

With tongs or chopsticks, dip the vegetables into the batter. Let drip for a moment and dip into the hot butter, frying until golden. Butter should be kept consistently at 365-370°.

Sauce:

Combine vegetable stock, tamari and lemon juice in saucepan. Heat.

Tempura should be served at once, with bowls of warm sauce sprinkled with grated ginger. This amount of vegetables should serve about 6.

PAKORAS

1 cup chick pea flour
1 cup rice flour
½ teaspoon cayenne
1 teaspoon turmeric
½ teaspoon salt
2 tablespoons buttermilk (optional)
1¾ to 2 cups water
bite-size pieces of vegetables such as carrots, onions,
    potatoes, mushrooms, spinach leaves, broccoli
clarified butter or oil for deep frying

Mix batter of first seven ingredients. Dip a piece of vegetable in the batter, coating it well, and drop into a pot of hot butter. Fry until pakora is a golden brown. Drain on paper towels and serve immediately with a chutney sauce (recipes pp. 240-241). Makes enough pakora batter for about 6 persons.

Variation:
    Some fruits, such as bananas, plantain, apples, pears, papaya, etc., may be used instead of, or in addition to, the vegetables. In this case, a sweet chutney may be desired.

MUNG SPROUT VEGETABLES

2 tablespoons clarified butter
1 teaspoon turmeric
1 teaspoon ground cumin
1 teaspoon cumin seeds
3 teaspoons ground coriander
1 teaspoon mustard seeds
1 medium-size onion, chopped
½ medium-size green pepper, chopped
2 medium-size potatoes, peeled and cubed
salt to taste
2 cups raw mung sprouts

Heat butter at medium temperature, preferably in a cast iron skillet. Add turmeric, ground cumin, cumin seed and ground coriander. Once thoroughly heated, add mustard seeds. When the mustard seeds begin to pop, add chopped onion. When onions are transparent, add green pepper. Fry for 5 minutes. Add potatoes and fry for another 5 minutes. Add salt to taste; wash and add mung sprouts. Cook over medium heat for 15 to 20 minutes until potatoes are tender, adding a little water if necessary. Serves 4.

VEGETARIAN JAMBALAYA

3 cups cooked rice
1 medium-size onion, diced
1 pound mushrooms, chopped
2 tablespoons clarified butter
2 medium-size green peppers, chopped
1 stalk celery, chopped
2 large tomatoes, peeled and chopped
½ teaspoon paprika
3 tablespoons chopped parsley
dash oregano
dash sweet basil
dash marjoram
dash thyme
½ cup melted butter

Cook rice. Saute onion and mushrooms in butter until onion is transparent. Combine all vegetables with the rice. Add seasonings and melted butter and mix well. Turn into a 1 quart casserole and bake, covered, at 300° for about 1 hour. Serves 4.

VEGETABLE PILAF

2 tablespoons clarified butter
½ cup finely chopped onion
2 teaspoons salt
1 cup basmati (natural white) rice
1 cup small cubes of potato
1 cup cubed cauliflower
½ medium-size green pepper, sliced paper-thin
½ cup fresh green peas
2½ cups water
1/8 teaspoon turmeric
1/8 teaspoon ground cumin
1/8 teaspoon ground coriander
1/8 teaspoon cayenne
dash cinnamon
dash ground cloves

Heat butter. Add onions and salt and stir constantly; fry for about 7 minutes or until onions are golden brown. Stir in rice; mix well. Add the rest of the ingredients and bring to a boil. Lower heat and cover. Steam over low heat for about 35 minutes or until water is evaporated and rice is tender. Serves 4.

VEGETABLE CURRY

¼ cup clarified butter
1½ teaspoons whole cumin seeds
2 cups chopped onion
1 large green pepper, chopped
1 tablespoon salt
1 tablespoon ground coriander
1 teaspoon turmeric
1 bay leaf
2 medium potatoes, diced (about 1½ cups)
¼ cup water
2 medium-size carrots, thinly sliced
2 cups cauliflower flowerettes (1 small head)
1½ cups fresh green peas
1 medium-size zucchini, thinly sliced
20 ounces garbanzo beans, cooked

Heat clarified butter at medium temperature in a large skillet. Fry cumin seeds until brown (about 45 seconds). Turn heat to medium-low and add onions, green pepper, salt, coriander, turmeric and bay leaf. Cook for 2 minutes. Add potatoes and water; cover and simmer on low heat for about 10 minutes. Add carrots and cauliflower; cover and simmer for 5 to 7 minutes. Add peas, zucchini and garbanzo beans; cover and simmer for another 10 minutes. Remove bay leaf. Serve with sauce. Makes 6 servings.

Sauce:
      2 cups plain yogurt
      1 large cucumber
      ¼ teaspoon salt
      1/8 teaspoon ground cumin

Peel cucumber, remove seeds and grate. Add yogurt, salt and cumin. Cover and refrigerate until chilled. Makes 2½ cups.

VEGETARIAN EGG ROLLS

2 cups mushrooms
2 medium scallions
1 small green pepper
3 medium-size leaves of bok choy
1 medium-size carrot
1 cup bamboo shoots
½ cup mung bean sprouts
¼ cup tamari sauce
1 teaspoon ground ginger
1 package egg roll skins
2 to 3 cups clarified butter or oil in a wok or deep
   pan for deep frying

Chop all the vegetables into small pieces except for
the carrots, which should be shredded. Place vegetables into
a large bowl and mix thoroughly. In a small bowl mix the
tamari sauce and ginger until smooth. Pour over the vegetables and mix until all the liquid has been absorbed.

Lay out an egg roll skin diagonally. Fill the center
with vegetables. Fold top down over vegetables, then sides,
then roll to the bottom point and seal with a touch of water.

Heat the clarified butter to about 375° and place
egg rolls into the butter. Cover; let deep fry for about 1
minute, then turn the rolls over and fry until a golden brown.
Drain egg rolls on paper towels. Delicious with a sweet and
sour sauce. Makes 12 egg rolls.

SWEET AND SOUR SAUCE

1 egg, beaten
1 cup milk
¼ cup milk powder
3 tomatoes, peeled, seeded and blended

94

¼ cup raw sugar
juice of 1 lemon
½ teaspoon ground ginger
¾ teaspoon dry mustard
pinch of salt

Combine egg, milk and milk powder in a double boiler. Heat until hot to the touch. Add sugar and blended tomatoes. Heat to hot once again. Add lemon juice and spices. Mix well and serve warm or chilled. Makes 2½ cups of sauce.

GREEN BEANS WITH COCONUT

2 pounds fresh green beans
3 tablespoons clarified butter
1 teaspoon salt
1 teaspoon turmeric
1/8 teaspoon cayenne
¼ cup fresh grated coconut
2 tablespoons fresh coconut milk
1 teaspoon ground coriander

Slice green beans lengthwise into four pieces.

In a skillet, heat the butter, add salt, turmeric and cayenne. Stir well, browning for a few seconds. Add the green beans and coat well with the spices. Cover pan and cook beans for about 5 minutes. Add the grated coconut, the coconut milk and the coriander.

Cover skillet and cook on low heat for about 5-10 minutes more.   If beans are too wet, cook a few more minutes without a cover. Serves 4-6.

Soups
and
Salads

ALPHABET SOUP

3 tablespoons kidney beans
3 tablespoons azuki beans
3 tablespoons pinto or white beans
3 tablespoons black or soy beans
3 tablespoons garbanzo or mung beans
4 tablespoons split peas, green or yellow
5 tablespoons lentils
2 tablespoons clarified butter
5 pureed tomatoes
1 large onion, chopped
2 stalks celery, chopped
2 tablespoons finely chopped parsley
1 teaspoon basil
1 bay leaf
salt to taste
1 cup whole wheat alphabet noodles

Wash beans well and soak overnight in 1 quart of water. The next day, cook the beans in the same water for 1 hour.

Add butter, vegetables and seasonings and cook for about 45 more minutes. Add noodles during the last ten minutes. Serves 4-6.

CELERY CHEESE SOUP

2 cups finely chopped celery
¼ cup butter, melted
3 cups water
1 teaspoon sea salt
¼ cup finely chopped parsley
3 cups milk
1 teaspoon sweet basil
1 teaspoon marjoram
1 teaspoon coriander
1 cup grated cheddar cheese
1 cup soy granules

Add celery to butter and simmer for about 15 minutes, covering the pot tightly to prevent browning. Add water, salt and parsley. Let simmer for another 15 minutes.

In a separate pan, heat the milk with the spices, but do not boil. Pour milk mixture into the celery mixture. (Oil will separate from the liquid at this point.) Gradually add grated cheese and soy granules, stirring until soup is thick. Serves 6.

CABBAGE SOUP

2½ pounds green cabbage, shredded
3 quarts water
2 tablespoons salt
2 cloves garlic
1 teaspoon caraway seeds
1 teaspoon black peppercorns
2 bay leaves
2 teaspoons oregano
1 pint water
½ cup unsalted butter, softened
½ cup flour
1 pint heavy cream
¾ cup grated mild cheddar cheese
dash of mace
salt and pepper to taste

Put cabbage, water and salt in a large kettle and bring to a boil. Reduce heat and simmer, covered, for one hour.

Make herb tea with garlic, caraway, peppercorns, bay leaves, oregano and a pint of water. Simmer tea for 15 minutes; let stand 10 more minutes to cool. Strain herbs and add tea to cabbage.

With your hands, combine softened butter and flour. When cabbage is done, add flour mixture, using wire whisk to stir. Continue stirring until smooth and thick—about 10 minutes. Add cream, cheese, mace and salt and pepper to taste. Makes 8-10 servings.

CARROT SOUP

10 medium-size carrots, peeled and cut into chunks
milk
1/8 teaspoon ginger
1/8 teaspoon cinnamon
1/8 teaspoon turmeric
¼ teaspoon ground cumin
½ teaspoon coriander
dash of nutmeg
2 tablespoons clarified butter
1 small onion, chopped
¼ cup chopped fresh parsley
basil, as desired
summer savory, as desired
salt and pepper to taste

Boil carrots in enough water to cover them. When cooked, place carrots in a blender with the water they were boiled in. Blend, adding milk as needed to get the desired thickness. (This soup is good fairly thin.) Return to the cooking pan and set aside.

In a cast-iron skillet, fry ginger, cinnamon, turmeric, cumin, coriander and nutmeg in butter. When hot, add onion and fry, stirring frequently, until it is translucent. Add a little water if necessary to keep from burning. Add parsley, basil and savory to taste. Cook for a minute more until the herbs are soft.

Add the spices to the blended carrots and bring to a boil. Add salt and pepper to taste. Makes about 8 servings.

ROOT SOUP

1 pound carrots, chopped
1 large turnip, chopped
1 pound potatoes, chopped
2 quarts vegetable stock
1 teaspoon sea salt
1 teaspoon peppercorns
3 tablespoons unsalted butter
½ pound onions, chopped
½ cup heavy cream
whole wheat croutons, sauteed in butter

Place carrots, turnip and potatoes in a kettle and cover with soup stock. Bring to a boil; reduce heat to simmer and cover. After a half hour add salt and peppercorns; cook for 45 more minutes, covered.

Melt butter in a skillet and add onions. Cook, covered, over low heat for half an hour.

Combine the carrot mixture and onions in a blender and puree. Return to the kettle and cook 15 more minutes. Whisk in heavy cream just before serving. Add croutons. Serves 8-10.

POTATO SOUP

3 tablespoons clarified butter
10 medium potatoes, peeled
milk
2 small onions, chopped
¾ cup sliced fresh mushrooms
½ cup chopped parsley
1 tablespoon basil
1 teaspoon chives, minced
½ teaspoon turmeric
2 teaspoons ground cumin
3 teaspoons ground coriander
salt and pepper to taste

Cut up the potatoes and place in a cooking pot, adding boiling water to cover; cook until tender. Place the potatoes and the cooking water in a blender; add milk as needed to blend potatoes to a smooth and thin consistency. Return to the cooking pot and set aside.

In a cast-iron skillet, fry turmeric, cumin and coriander in butter, stirring frequently, until the spices start to turn dark. Add onions and mushrooms; fry and stir until onions are translucent and mushrooms are soft. (Adding salt to the mushrooms while they are cooking will cause them to let go of moisture. This will help avoid burning. Add water if necessary.) When onions and mushrooms are cooked, add parsley and basil. Cook until the herbs are soft.

Add this mixture to the blended potatoes and milk; bring to a boil. Add salt and pepper to taste. Serve hot.
Makes about 8 servings.

SOY-POTATO SOUP

4 medium potatoes
2 tablespoons butter
½ cup soy granules
1 teaspoon oregano
1 teaspoon ground cumin
1 teaspoon marjoram
½ cup milk
3 cups water

Cut up potatoes, cover with water and cook slowly until soft. Beat until smooth. Add butter, soy granules, spices and liquids. Cook at medium temperature for 15 minutes. Serves 6.

Note: If you prefer thick soup, you can increase the amount of soy granules and milk while decreasing the amount of water.

CREAM OF SPINACH SOUP

2 quarts of water
3 medium-size potatoes, diced
1 onion, chopped
1 teaspoon salt
4 cups fresh spinach, chopped
½ pint sour cream
2½ tablespoons cornstarch or arrowroot
¼ cup water
salt and freshly ground black pepper to taste

Add potatoes, onion and salt to 2 quarts of water. Bring to a boil; turn heat to low and simmer until the potatoes are soft.

Add spinach to the potato mixture; cover and cook for about 5 minutes more.

In a small bowl, mix sour cream, cornstarch and water until smooth and without any lumps. Add the sour cream mixture to the soup. Bring to a boil, stirring occasionally, until the soup thickens. Add salt and pepper to taste. Serves 8.

Variation:

Chopped green beans, asparagus, or broccoli may be substituted for the spinach.

SPICED SPINACH SOUP

1 heaping teaspoon turmeric
1½ teaspoons ground cumin
2 teaspoons ground coriander
4 tablespoons clarified butter
1 pound fresh spinach, cleaned
2 small onions, chopped
½ clove garlic
2 quarts milk
1 teaspoon salt
juice of ½ lemon

Fry butter and spices in a large pan or cast-iron skillet until browned.

Place spinach, onion, garlic and a little milk in a blender and blend until liquid. Keep adding milk until blender is full and all is whipped. Pour spinach mixture into the pan with the spices and turn on high heat. Add the rest of the milk and the salt and mix well. Add lemon juice and stir. When soup begins to boil, turn down and simmer, covered, until the raw smell disappears and the green color becomes dark and rich. Serves 6-8.

HIGH PROTEIN CREAM OF MUSHROOM SOUP

2 pounds fresh mushrooms, sliced
1 large onion, sliced
2 cloves garlic, pressed
7 tablespoons butter
3 tablespoons whole wheat flour
¼ cup soy flour
milk as needed
1 teaspoon vegetable seasoning
salt to taste
a few sprigs of parsley, minced
½ cup instant dry milk

Saute mushrooms, onion and garlic in 2 tablespoons of the butter until tender but not brown. Set aside to cool. Put mushroom mixture through food processor or colander. Set aside.

In heavy saucepan melt 5 tablespoons butter. Add the two types of flour and make a roux. Cook over low heat and add milk until a thick white sauce is attained. Add spices and salt as well as herbs and parsley. To this, add the mushroom mixture and adjust the consistency with milk, if necessary. Add the powdered milk and stir until creamy.

Serve with whole wheat bread or croutons. Serves 6-8.

Note: This soup is a complete protein.

SPLIT PEA SOUP

1 cup green or yellow split peas, washed
1 large onion, chopped
2 or 3 stalks celery, cut up (include the tops)
3 carrots, scraped and sliced
1 large potato, cubed
fresh parsley, minced

Using a large kettle and enough water so that the peas do not stick, simmer all ingredients except parsley until the peas begin to lose their shape—about 1½ hours.

Season to taste with sea salt. Sprinkle each serving with minced parsley. Serves 6.

Variation:
½ cup of rice or millet may be substituted for the potato.

FRESH GREEN PEA SOUP

4 cups shelled fresh peas
½ cup coarsely chopped leeks
½ cup water
2 sprigs fresh mint or ½ teaspoon dried
1 teaspoon salt
½ teaspoon crumbled leaf chervil
½ teaspoon sweet basil
¼ teaspoon crumbled leaf marjoram
¼ teaspoon thyme
¼ teaspoon white pepper
1 tablespoon sugar (optional)
1½ quarts milk, at room temperature

Combine peas, leek and water in a medium-size saucepan; bring just to boiling, but do not boil.

In a blender, whirl peas and liquid, mint leaves, salt, chervil, basil, marjoram, thyme, white pepper, sugar and a small amount of the milk until smooth.

Pour mixture into saucepan; add remaining milk. Heat thoroughly. Garnish with fresh mint sprigs, if you wish. Serves 6.

BLACK BEAN SOUP

1 cup black beans
1½ quarts cold water
1 onion, chopped
1 tablespoon clarified butter
1 sprig fresh parsley
2 tablespoons lemon juice
½ teaspoon dry mustard
salt and pepper
2 tablespoons butter
2 tablespoons unbleached flour
yogurt
paprika

Soak the beans overnight. Drain them and cover with the cold water. Saute onion in the clarified butter. Add onion, parsley, lemon juice and mustard to the beans and simmer until the beans are soft, adding more water if needed. Season with salt and pepper. Pour mixture into a blender and puree.

In another saucepan, make a roux of butter and flour. Add to blender with the bean soup and blend again. Simmer soup for 15 more minutes. Serve soup in bowl with a dollop of yogurt sprinkled with paprika. Serves 4.

PINTO BEAN STEW

1 cup pinto beans
4 cups water
2 medium-size onions, chopped
¼ cup clarified butter
1 zucchini, peeled and sliced in ½ inch pieces
1 stalk broccoli, peeled and sliced in ½ inch pieces
2 stalks celery, thinly sliced
3 large tomatoes, peeled and chopped
2 carrots, peeled and thinly sliced
¼ cup millet
¼ cup rice
2 teaspoons salt
1 teaspoon pepper
1 vegetable bouillon cube
½ stick butter

Cook pinto beans in water until soft. Brown onions in clarified butter in a large stew pot. Add beans, other ingredients, and enough water to fill pot; bring to a boil. Reduce heat and simmer for 40 to 45 minutes until vegetables are tender and rice and millet are cooked. Taste for seasoning. Serves 4.

PUMPKIN SOUP

1 cup chopped green onions
2 tablespoons butter
2 cups mashed pumpkin or squash
1 cup soup stock
1 cup grated carrots
½ teaspoon salt
dash nutmeg
1 cup light cream

Saute onion in butter over low heat until tender. Add pumpkin, soup stock, carrots, salt and nutmeg. Simmer, covered, for 20 minutes. Stir in cream and serve. Serves 4-6.

QUICK BORSCH

1 large beet
4 to 5 tablespoons plain yogurt
nutmeg

Dice beet, cover with water, and cook until soft. Mash beets in the water and add yogurt. Cook a few seconds to warm yogurt. Serve in bowls, sprinkled with nutmeg. Serves 4.

VEGETABLE BROTH

4 onions, coarsely chopped
4 carrots, diced
4 ribs celery with leaves, coarsely chopped
4 parsnips, diced
2 turnips, diced
4 tablespoons butter
1/3 cup chopped parsley
2 teaspoons peppercorns
2 bay leaves
½ teaspoon basil
½ teaspoon thyme
3½ teaspoons salt
3 quarts water

In large kettle slowly saute onions, carrots, celery, parsnips and turnips in butter for 15 minutes or until almost tender. Tie parsley, peppercorns, bay leaves, basil and thyme in a 6 x 6 inch piece of cheesecloth. Add to pot with salt and water. Bring to boil, cover, and simmer 3 hours. Strain broth. Makes 8 to 10 cups.

Note: Use as a base for sauces and soups or for cooking grains. Good as a first course or as a meal with bread and cheese.

TOMATO YOGURT SOUP

2 pounds ripe tomatoes
2 cups yogurt
1 garlic clove, pressed
¼ teaspoon celery salt
1/8 teaspoon turmeric
1/8 teaspoon cumin
1/8 teaspoon cayenne
¼ teaspoon coriander
juice of 1 lemon
salt and pepper to taste
yogurt and chopped chives for garnish

In blender, puree tomatoes after having removed the skins. Add the remaining ingredients to the blender except the garnish and whip. Put in a saucepan and bring to a boil. Cover and simmer for 5 minutes. Remove from heat and allow to cool. Chill in refrigerator and serve with a dollop of yogurt and a sprinkling of chives in each bowl. Serves 6.

MISO SOUP

1 teaspoon sesame oil
1 onion, sliced
pinch of sea salt
5 cups water
2 cups chopped greens
1 carrot, sliced
¼ cup miso soybean paste

Place soup pot on medium heat and add oil. When oil is hot add onions; stir for 2 to 5 minutes until slightly transparent. Add salt, water and remaining vegetables and bring to a boil. Reduce heat and simmer, covered, for 20 to 30 minutes or until vegetables are just tender. Remove from heat. Dilute miso with about ¼ cup of the soup broth and stir into the soup. Cover pot and allow to steep for about 5 minutes before serving. (Miso should not be boiled as this destroys its valuable digestion-aiding enzymes.) Serves 4.

TAMARI SOUP

1 clove garlic, crushed
1 teaspoon chopped parsley
¼ cup clarified butter
½ cup diced broccoli
½ cup diced mushrooms
½ cup diced asparagus
¼ cup diced celery
¼ cup chopped onion
4 cups water
about ½ cup tamari sauce
¼ cup sesame seeds
salt and pepper

Saute garlic and parsley in butter. Add vegetables and water to cover; steam for 5 minutes. Add 4 cups water. Starting with 1/3 cup tamari, add until the flavor suits you. Add sesame seeds and salt and pepper to taste. Makes 6½ cups.

ROSE HIPS SOUP

2 cups dried rose hips
1½ quarts water
1½ teaspoons cornstarch
½ cup raw sugar
whipped cream (optional)
2 tablespoons ground almonds (optional)

Crush the rose hips. Bring water just to a boil; add rose hips. Cover and simmer 45 minutes, stirring occasionally.

Strain through a sieve into a large pot, adding enough water to make 1½ quarts. Mix cornstarch with a small amount of water; add this and sugar to the soup. Simmer for 3 minutes. Pour into bowls and top with whipped cream and ground almonds, if desired. Serve hot or chilled. Serves 4-6.

CRANBERRY SOUP

6 cups cranberry juice
2/3 cup raw sugar
1/3 cup cold water
3 tablespoons potato starch
whipped cream, as desired

Combine juice and sugar in a saucepan. Heat until almost boiling; remove from heat.

Mix cold water and potato starch. Slowly pour potato starch mixture into juice, stirring constantly with a wire whisk. Return to heat and bring almost to a boil, stirring constantly. Simmer one or two minutes until soup thickens and becomes transparent. Pour into a bowl and serve with a dollop of fresh-whipped cream. Serves 4-6.

FRUIT SOUP

1 cup dried apricots
1 cup sweet prunes, pitted
½ cup dates, pitted
¼ cup dried currants or seedless raisins
½ lemon, sliced paper thin
6 cups water
pinch of salt
4 sticks of cinnamon
3 tablespoons minute tapioca or cornstarch or arrowroot
1 cup peeled and diced tart apple

Put all the dried fruit in a saucepan. Add the lemon, water, salt and cinnamon. Mix the tapioca with a little water until dissolved and add to the fruit. Cover pan and bring to a boil. Reduce heat and cook for 20 minutes. Add the apple, cover and simmer for 8 or 10 minutes more. Serve hot or cold. Serves 8.

Variation:
    Fresh peaches and apricots may be used in season. They should be added with the apple during the last stage of cooking.

CARROT RAISIN APPLE SALAD

10 carrots, peeled and grated
1 cup seedless raisins
½ cup chopped walnuts
1½ to 2 cups plain yogurt
2 tablespoons honey (optional)
3 apples, peeled and chopped

Mix all ingredients together and serve with fresh sprouts and sunflower seeds on top. Makes about 6 servings.

ROMAINE SPINACH SALAD

2 cups romaine lettuce, cut in narrow strips
2 cups fresh spinach, cut in narrow strips
4 carrots, peeled and grated
4 stalks celery, finely sliced
4 hard cooked eggs, chopped
2 apples, peeled and chopped
½ cup homemade cheese (recipe p. 6)
juice of 1 lemon
1 cup buttermilk
1 teaspoon roasted, ground cumin
salt and pepper to taste

Mix lettuce, spinach, carrots, celery, eggs, apples and cheese. Squeeze lemon juice over all; toss with buttermilk. Sprinkle on cumin and salt and pepper to taste and toss again. Makes about 6 servings.

AVOCADO CHEESE SALAD

10 hard boiled eggs, chopped
2 avocados, cubed
1 cup ricotta cheese
½ cup yogurt
1 tablespoon finely chopped chives
1 teaspoon onion powder
1 teaspoon celery seed
1 tablespoon salt
1 teaspoon pepper
¼ cup finely chopped celery
2 tomatoes, cubed
1 teaspoon dill seed

Mix all ingredients together and serve cold. Makes about 8 servings.

Variation:
Try adding sunflower seeds and a dash of tamari sauce to the above ingredients.

121

GREEN PEA SALAD I

Per person:
    1 cup frozen peas (thaw under cold water)
    2 tablespoons cold pressed oil
    ¼ cup lemon juice
    ½ teaspoon salt
    1 teaspoon crumbled dry or minced fresh mint
    2 tablespoons finely diced celery
    ¼ cup yogurt, sour cream or kefir cheese

Garnish:
    cucumber slices
    tomato wedges
    sliced, hard-cooked eggs

Mix peas, oil, lemon juice, salt, mint and celery. Chill at least 2 hours. When ready to serve, stir in yogurt. Place on plate, garnish as desired and serve with toast or muffins. Serves 1.

GREEN PEA SALAD II

Per person:
  ½ cup frozen peas (thaw under cold water)
  ½ cup shredded cheddar cheese
  1 cup lettuce pieces
  1 tablespoon finely chopped scallion or green onion
  2 tablespoons sesame seeds
  ½ teaspoon salt
  1 teaspoon parsley
  ¼ cup homemade mayonnaise (recipe p. 128)
  1 tablespoon lemon juice
  dash of pepper

  Mix all ingredients thoroughly. Chill and serve. Serves
1.

BULGUR MINT SALAD

½ cup cracked wheat (bulgur)
½ cup chopped fresh mint leaves
½ cup chopped fresh Italian parsley leaves
3 scallions, white part only, finely chopped
1½ tablespoons lemon juice
1½ tablespoons sesame oil or other cold pressed oil
pinch of salt
freshly ground pepper

Soak cracked wheat in water to cover for 20 minutes. Drain through a sieve, pressing out as much water as possible. Dry on a clean towel. Combine in a serving bowl with all remaining ingredients, using more lemon juice or oil if you like. Serves 4.

Variation:

If fresh mint is not available, substitute fresh watercress or fresh mung sprouts.

STEAMED VEGETABLE SALAD

1 large or 2 medium-size carrots, peeled
6 to 8 asparagus spears, trimmed
1 large stalk broccoli, peeled
juice of 1 lemon
½ cup frozen corn, thawed in cold water
1 cup frozen peas, thawed in cold water
2 large tomatoes, cut in wedges
2 cups lettuce pieces
1 cucumber, peeled and sliced very thin
1 cup homemade mayonnaise (recipe p. 128)
1 small onion, chopped
2 tablespoons parsley
1 teaspoon salt
½ teaspoon pepper

Slice carrots, asparagus and broccoli into bite-sized pieces and steam until tender. Toss with lemon juice and chill. Mix well with remaining ingredients and serve. Serves 6.

TABOOLEY SALAD

1 cup cracked wheat (bulgur)
¼ cup roasted soy grits (optional)
2 cups boiling water
¼ cup cold pressed oil
1 cup chopped parsley
3 green onions, finely chopped
6 tablespoons lemon juice
3 tomatoes, peeled
hard-boiled egg, finely chopped

Soak bulgur and soy grits in boiling water for about 30 minutes. Drain well and add oil, parsley, onions and lemon juice. Cover and refrigerate. To serve, toss again and garnish with tomato wedges and chopped egg. Serves 4.

Variation:
　　　Lime juice may be substituted for lemon juice.
　　　1 tablespoon brewer's yeast may be added to bulgur.

TOFU SALAD DRESSING

¼ cup raw sunflower seeds, ground
juice of 4 medium-size lemons
2 cups tofu
2 tablespoons tamari or soy sauce
¼ cup water, or to desired consistency
¼ teaspoon salt
freshly ground black pepper

Grind sunflower seeds in coffee mill or blender until ground to a fine meal. Add lemon juice and tofu. Blend until well mixed. Add tamari sauce and water until desired consistency is reached. Season with salt and pepper.

Variations:
Use cashews instead of the sunflower seeds. Some walnuts and almonds can be added for a sweeter taste.
Add ½ teaspoon of ground roasted cumin and a pinch of cayenne.

MAYONNAISE

1 egg
juice of 1 lemon
1 tablespoon green onion, minced
1 teaspoon salt
1 cup cold pressed oil

Put egg in blender. Add lemon juice, onion and salt.
Start blender, using a medium speed. Add ¼ cup of oil very
slowly drop by drop. Then add ¾ cup of oil gradually. When
thickened and oil is used up, remove from blender and chill.

YOGURT DRESSING

1 cup yogurt
1 tablespoon lemon juice
1 teaspoon onion powder
pinch of dill
1 teaspoon chopped chives
pinch of salt
honey to taste

Mix all ingredients in blender. Chill.

POPPY SEED DRESSING

1 cup cold pressed oil
¼ cup lemon juice
1½ teaspoons turmeric
½ to 1½ teaspoons mustard powder
¼ cup poppy seeds
1/8 cup honey
½ teaspoon salt

Mix well and chill. Serve over crisp salads.

QUICK FRENCH DRESSING

¾ cup cold pressed oil
½ cup lemon juice
2 tablespoons ground sesame seeds
2 to 3 tablespoons honey
½ teaspoon tahini
1 teaspoon paprika
2 teaspoons onion powder
salt to taste

Mix well in blender or jar. Chill and serve.

ITALIAN DRESSING

3 parts cold pressed oil
1 part lemon juice
1/8 part salt
dash onion powder
dash of tahini
bit of sliced garlic

Mix well and chill. Remove garlic, shake and serve.

Breads

FOUR FLOUR BREAD

½ cup yellow corn meal
1/3 cup brown sugar
1 tablespoon salt
2 cups boiling water
¼ cup clarified butter or oil
2 packages active dry yeast
½ cup lukewarm water
1¾ cups stirred whole wheat flour
¾ cup stirred rye flour
3¼ cups sifted unbleached flour

Thoroughly combine the corn meal, sugar, salt, boiling water and butter. Let cool to lukewarm, about thirty minutes.

Soften yeast in ½ cup lukewarm water. Stir into the corn meal mixture. Add the whole wheat and rye flours; mix well. Stir in enough unbleached flour to make a moderately stiff dough. Turn out on a lightly floured surface and knead until smooth and elastic—6 to 8 minutes. Place in greased bowl, turning once to grease surface. Cover and let rise in warm place until double—50 to 60 minutes.

Punch down; turn out on lightly floured surface and divide in half. Cover and let rest 10 minutes. Shape into two loaves and place in greased 9 x 5 x 3 inch loaf pans. Let rise again until almost double—about 30 minutes. Bake in 375° oven for 45 minutes of until done. Cool on rack. Makes 2 loaves.

NO-KNEAD WHOLE WHEAT BREAD

4 teaspoons dry yeast
2/3 cup warm water
2 tablespoons plus 2 teaspoons molasses
5 cups whole wheat flour
2/3 cup warm water
1 tablespoon salt
1/3 cup wheat germ
1 1/3 cups lukewarm water
1 teaspoon butter
1 teaspoon sesame seeds

Combine yeast, water and 2 teaspoons of the molasses. Warm flour in 250° oven for 20 minutes. Combine rest of molasses and 2/3 cup warm water. Combine yeast mixture with molasses mixture. Stir this into warmed flour, then add salt, wheat germ and 1 1/3 cups warm water.

Butter a standard loaf pan (9 x 5 x 3 inches); turn dough into pan. Sprinkle sesame seeds over the top. Let rise until loaves are 1/3 more than their original size—about 50 minutes.

Preheat oven to 425°. Bake about 50 minutes or until done. Makes 1 loaf.

MA'S BREAD

1 package dry yeast
½ cup warm water
2 tablespoons salt
1 cup cracked wheat cereal
¾ cup boiling water
3 cups warm water
1½ cups whole wheat flour
¼ cup corn meal
unbleached flour

Dissolve yeast in ½ cup warm water. Put into mixing bowl with salt, cracked wheat and boiling water. Let stand for 5 minutes. Then add warm water, whole wheat flour and corn meal. Add enough unbleached flour to make a batter; beat lightly. Add more unbleached flour until dough is stiff and pulls away from the bowl. Turn out on a board and let rest, covered, for 10 minutes.

Lightly grease a bowl and three bread pans. Knead dough about 10 minutes, adding flour as needed until dough is smooth and elastic. Place in bowl; turn to grease top, cover, and let rise for about 2 hours—until double in size.

Punch down; divide into three pieces. Let rest for 10 minutes. Shape into loaves. Place into buttered 9 x 5 x 3 inch pans, cover, and let rise until double—about 45 minutes. Bake at 400° for 10 minutes, and then at 375° for 50 to 60 minutes. Makes 3 loaves.

OAT BREAD

2½ cups whole wheat flour
2 cups oats
1½ teaspoons baking soda
½ cup butter, melted
2½ cups milk, scalded
½ teaspoon sea salt
½ teaspoon vegetable salt
sesame seeds

Mix oats, flour and soda. Add melted butter, then the milk. Stir in salts. Pour into two buttered loaf pans and sprinkle tops with sesame seeds. Bake at 300° for 1½ hours. Cool well before slicing. Makes 2 loaves.

Variation:
Eliminate vegetable salt and increase sea salt to 1 teaspoon. Add 1/3 cup raw sugar. Spread in a 15 x 10 inch oblong pan and bake at 300 to 325° for 50 minutes or until firm and golden brown. This becomes a sweet bread.

IRISH SODA BREAD

2 cups whole wheat flour
2 cups unsifted, unbleached flour
1 teaspoon salt
3 teaspoons baking powder
1 teaspoon baking soda
¼ cup raw sugar (optional)
1/8 - 1/4 teaspoon ground cardamom or coriander
2 cups dried currants or raisins
¼ cup butter
1 egg
1¾ cups buttermilk

Combine the flours, salt, baking powder, soda, sugar and spice in a large bowl. Add butter and cut in with a pastry blender or two knives until crumbly. Beat egg slightly and mix with buttermilk; add to dry ingredients and stir until blended. Turn out on a floured board and knead until smooth, 2 to 3 minutes.

Divide dough in half, and shape each into a round loaf. Place each loaf in a buttered 8-inch cake or pie pan; press down until dough fills pans. With a sharp knife, cut a large cross on the top of each loaf, about ½ inch deep in the middle. Bake in a moderately hot oven (375°) for 35 to 40 minutes. Makes 2 loaves.

Variation:

¼ teaspoon cinnamon and a dash of allspice may be substituted for the cardamom, if you prefer.

APPLE BANANA BREAD

1 cup milk
½ cup tofu
3 medium-size, very ripe bananas
4 cups sifted unbleached flour
2 teaspoons baking powder
2/3 cup butter, softened
1 teaspoon salt
2 teaspoons cinnamon
1 teaspoon nutmeg
1 cup maple syrup
4 eggs, separated
5 medium-size apples, peeled and grated

Put milk, tofu and bananas in blender. Blend until smooth. Combine all ingredients, except apples and egg whites. Mix well on medium speed of mixer until batter is smooth. Stir in grated apple. Beat egg whites until stiff. Fold into batter. Pour into three small oiled loaf pans.

Bake at 350° for 1 hour or until a toothpick inserted in the center comes out clean. If the tops brown too quickly, cover with a sheet of foil. Makes 3 loaves.

Note: This recipe works well with rice flour as well as wheat flour.

APPLESAUCE BREAD

2 envelopes active dry yeast
1/3 cup warm water
2 teaspoons salt
1 tablespoon cinnamon
3 tablespoons molasses
2 cups warm applesauce
1 cup raisins, plumped in hot water and drained
3 to 3½ cups unbleached flour
3 cups whole wheat flour

In a large bowl of mixer dissolve yeast in warm water. Add salt, cinnamon, molasses, applesauce and raisins. Add unbleached flour. Beat at high speed until smooth. Cover with a towel and let rise in warm, draft-free place for 15 minutes. Mixture should begin to bubble.

Set aside 1 cup of whole wheat flour for kneading. Beat in the remaining flour to form a soft, elastic dough. Sprinkle reserved cup of flour on a clean surface. Turn out the dough, cover with the bowl, and let rest for 15 minutes.

Knead for about 10 minutes. Place in a greased bowl, turn to grease top, cover, and let rise in a warm place until doubled, about 1 hour. Punch down and knead until smooth. Divide in half and shape into 2 loaves. Place in buttered loaf pans (9 x 5 x 3 inches) and let rise about 30 minutes. Bake in a preheated 375° oven for 35 to 40 minutes. Remove to racks and brush with butter. Makes 2 loaves.

UNSWEETENED BANANA BREAD

2½ cups yellow or white cornmeal
½ cup buckwheat flour
¾ cup millet flour
1½ teaspoons salt
4 teaspoons baking powder
¾ teaspoon nutmeg
1½ teaspoons arrowroot powder
4 medium-size bananas, mashed
½ cup melted butter
3 to 4 cups milk

Mix dry ingredients; combine bananas, butter and milk and add to dry mixture. Stir until evenly moistened. Spread in a buttered 9 x 13 inch pan or in two small bread pans and bake in a preheated 375° oven for 30 to 40 minutes. Makes 12 or more servings.

PEAR BREAD

2 cups yellow or white cornmeal
1½ cups whole wheat pastry flour
½ cup soy flour
1½ teaspoons salt
1 tablespoon baking powder
¾ teaspoon anise
¼ teaspoon mace
¼ teaspoon nutmeg
½ teaspoon cinnamon
3 eggs
3½ to 4 cups milk
6 pears, peeled and chopped

Mix dry ingredients together. Beat eggs; add milk and pear pieces. Combine wet and dry ingredients and mix until smooth. Bake in either muffin tins or in 2 small bread pans (well-greased) at 375° for 20 to 35 minutes.

PRUNE BREAD

½ pound of prunes (1½ cups cooked)
3 cups whole wheat pastry flour
¼ cup soy flour
½ cup millet flour
1½ teaspoons salt
4 teaspoons baking powder
1½ teaspoons cinnamon
1¼ cups prune juice (from the cooked prunes)
1 cup raisin juice (from soaked or boiled raisins)
2 eggs, beaten

Bring prunes to a boil with water just to cover. Boil about 10 to 15 minutes. Remove from heat. Mix dry ingredients together and set aside.

Remove prunes from the liquid and blend to a smooth consistency. Measure 1½ cups into a mixing bowl. Add 1¼ cups prune water, raisin water and beaten eggs. Mix wet and dry ingredients and bake in a buttered 9 x 13 inch pan at 375° for 30 to 45 minutes. Makes about 12 servings.

COCONUT BREAD

1 cup shredded fresh coconut or coconut flakes
4 cups milk
1 cup raisins
2 cups whole wheat pastry flour
1 cup cornmeal
½ cup rolled oats
½ cup soy flour (or powder)
1 tablespoon baking powder
1½ teaspoons salt
1 teaspoon ginger
¼ teaspoon mace

Soak coconut overnight in 2 cups of the milk. Then blend to make coconut milk.

Add remaining 2 cups of milk and the raisins. Mix remaining ingredients together and add to the liquid mixture; mix until smooth.

Pour into a buttered 9 x 13 inch pan and bake for 30 to 45 minutes in a 375° oven. Makes 12 or more servings.

PEACH NUT BREAD

2 cups whole wheat flour
2 teaspoons baking powder
½ teaspoon salt
¼ teaspoon cloves
2/3 cup brown sugar
½ teaspoon baking soda
½ teaspoon cinnamon
2 tablespoons softened butter
½ cup orange juice
2 eggs
2 cups diced peaches
½ cup chopped nutmeats

Sift dry ingredients into a large mixer bowl. Add butter, juice and eggs. Beat two minutes at medium speed, scraping bowl occasionally. By hand, fold in diced peaches and nuts.

Spread batter in a 9 x 5 x 3 inch greased and floured bread pan or two smaller pans. Bake one hour at 300° or until it tests done. Cool in pan for 15 minutes, then finish cooling on a rack. Makes one large or 2 small loaves.

PUMPKIN NUT BREAD

2 cups whole wheat flour
2½ teaspoons baking powder
½ teaspoon baking soda
1 teaspoon salt
1½ teaspoons cinnamon
½ teaspoon nutmeg
¼ teaspoon allspice
1 cup fresh pumpkin pulp
½ cup raw sugar
½ cup molasses
½ cup milk
2 eggs
¼ cup butter, softened
1 cup chopped walnuts or pecans

Soft together flour, baking powder, soda, salt and spices. Combine pumpkin, sugar, molasses, milk and eggs in a mixing bowl. Add dry ingredients and softened butter; mix until well blended. Stir in nuts.

Spread in a well-greased standard (9 x 5 x 3 inch) loaf pan. Bake in a 350° oven for 45 to 55 minutes or until toothpick inserted in center comes out clean. Makes 1 loaf.

Variation:

In place of the chopped walnuts, add ½ cup of roasted sunflower seeds and ½ cup of roasted sesame seeds.

STRAWBERRY BREAD

2 cups whole wheat pastry flour
1½ cups bran flakes
1½ teaspoons baking powder
2 teaspoons cinnamon
¼ teaspoon allspice
½ teaspoon salt
½ teaspoon baking soda
1 cup raw sugar
3 tablespoons wheat germ
¼ cup blanched and chopped almonds
¼ cup chopped walnuts
¼ cup chopped pumpkin seeds
1 egg
2 tablespoons clarified butter or cold pressed oil
1¼ cups fresh orange juice with pulp
1 cup sliced fresh strawberries

In a large bowl mix all the dry ingredients including nuts and seeds; set aside. In a small mixing bowl beat egg well. Add butter, orange juice and strawberries, mixing well. Combine with dry ingredients and blend.

Bake in a greased 9 x 5 x 3 inch loaf pan at 325° for 70 to 75 minutes or until bread tests done with a toothpick. Cool in the pan for 10 to 15 minutes; remove to racks. Serve warm or cold. Makes 1 loaf.

WHOLE WHEAT SCONES

2 cups whole wheat flour
2½ teaspoons baking powder
¼ teaspoon baking soda
½ teaspoon salt
6 tablespoons butter
1 large egg
½ cup buttermilk
milk

Heat oven to 425°. Sift flour, baking powder, baking soda and salt into a large bowl. Stir to mix well. Add butter and cut in with a pastry blender until the mixture resembles coarse corn meal. In a small bowl beat egg with a fork; stir in buttermilk. Add all at once to the dry ingredients and mix lightly with a fork until mixture clings together and forms a ball of soft dough.

Turn out dough on a lightly floured board and knead for about 6 turns. Handle dough lightly. With a rolling pin, roll out dough ½ inch thick. Dip a glass or biscuit cutter in flour and cut out biscuits close together. Pat dough scraps together and cut out.

Place biscuits on an ungreased baking sheet, about 1 inch apart for crusty sides, close together for soft sides. Brush tops of biscuits with milk. Bake for 10 minutes, or until golden brown. Serve warm with butter. Yields about 12 scones.

SCOTCH SCONES

1 cup graham flour
½ teaspoon cream of tartar
1 teaspoon baking soda
¼ teaspoon salt
¼ cup unsalted butter
1/3 cup light cream

Preheat oven to 400°.

Mix flour, cream of tartar, baking soda and salt. Cut in the butter until the mixture is moderately fine. Stir in the cream.

Pat gently (do not roll) into a circular mound that is ½ inch thick at the edge and 1½ to 2 inches thick at the center. Cut into 4 equal triangular pieces. Place well apart on a lightly oiled baking sheet. Brush with cream.

Bake for 15 minutes, until browned on top. Serve hot, with honey. Serves 4.

Variation:

Add ¼ to ½ cup of dried black currents to the dough.

GERMAN HOLIDAY LOAVES
(Hutzelbrot)

2 tablespoons dry yeast
2 cups sweet cider, lukewarm
7 cups rye flour
4 cups whole wheat flour
½ teaspoon salt
¾ cup unsweetened prune juice
¾ cup pear nectar or pear puree
1 pound seedless raisins
1 pound dried currants
1 cup pitted and chopped dates
rind of 3 oranges, grated
rind of 3 lemons, grated
1 cup split and blanched almonds
2 tablespoons ground cinnamon
1 teaspoon ground cloves
1 teaspoon ground allspice
½ cup unsweetened grape juice
1 egg yolk

Soften yeast in cider. Add 4 cups of the rye flour, 2 cups of the wheat flour and the salt. Mix well. Let mixture rise in a warm place for about 4 hours. Add prune juice and pear nectar. Meanwhile, soak fruits, rinds, nuts and spices in grape juice. Add them to the mixture. Stir in enough of the remaining flours to make a stiff dough. Knead.

Shape in 4 to 5 round loaves (about 2 pounds each) and place on oiled, floured cooky sheets. Set in a warm place to rise. When loaves are 1/3 larger than their original size, brush with egg yolk diluted in cold water and bake at 350° for about 1 hour and 20 minutes. Makes 4 or 5 loaves.

Note: This cake will improve with age and will keep for a long time.

RAISIN NUT BREAD

2 cups seedless raisins
1 cup water
4 cups whole wheat flour
1 tablespoon baking soda
1 teaspoon salt
2 cups raw sugar
¼ cup clarified butter or cold pressed oil
4 eggs
2 teaspoons vanilla
2 cups mashed bananas
2 cups coarsely chopped walnuts

Combine raisins and water in a medium-size saucepan; bring to a boil. Turn off heat and allow to cool. Combine whole wheat flour, baking soda and salt; set aside.

Beat sugar, butter, eggs and vanilla in a large bowl until blended. Drain raisins and add with bananas and nuts to the sugar mixture. Add flour mixture, stirring just to blend all the ingredients. Divide batter equally into two lightly oiled 9 x 5 x 3 inch baking pans.

Bake in a moderate oven (325°) for 1 hour. Lower oven temperature to very slow (250°) and continue to bake an additional 30 minutes or until a wooden toothpick inserted in the center comes out clean. The bread will be dark. Makes 2 loaves.

APRICOT POPPINS

2 cups sifted unbleached flour
½ cup raw sugar
3 teaspoons baking powder
½ teaspoon salt
1¼ cups dried apricots, washed and cut into ¼ inch
   pieces
¼ cup melted butter
1 egg, beaten
1 cup milk

Topping:

½ cup unbleached flour
¼ teaspoon ground cinnamon
1/3 cup date sugar or fructose
¼ cup melted butter

Sift together flour, sugar, baking powder and salt. Add 1 cup of the apricot pieces. Combine butter, egg and milk; add to dry ingredients. Mix until just blended.

Fill greased muffin tins 2/3 full. Place remaining apricot pieces on top of each. For topping, blend flour, cinnamon and date sugar into melted butter. Bake at 375° for 30 minutes or until lightly browned. Makes 18 muffins.

CARROT COCONUT MUFFINS

2 cups whole wheat flour
2 teaspoons baking powder
½ teaspoon salt
¼ to ½ cup raw sugar
½ cup grated carrot
1 cup grated coconut
1 egg, beaten
¼ cup clarified butter or cold pressed oil
1½ cups milk

Combine dry ingredients. Combine remaining ingredients in separate bowl. Fold wet and dry ingredients together quickly, just until flour is moistened. Spoon into greased muffin tin. Bake at 400° for about 20 minutes. Makes 12 muffins.

ORANGE ALMOND MUFFINS

2 cups whole wheat flour
4 teaspoons baking powder
½ teaspoon salt
¼ cup raw sugar
2 eggs, slightly beaten
1 cup milk
1 tablespoon grated orange rind
1 tablespoon orange juice
3 tablespoons melted butter
½ cup chopped almonds

Mix flour, baking powder, salt and sugar. Mix eggs, milk, orange rind, juice and butter. Add liquid to flour mixture, stirring only until all flour is dampened. Spoon into greased muffin tin and top with chopped nuts.

Bake in a hot oven (425°) for 25 minutes or until a toothpick comes out clean. Makes 12 muffins.

LUSCIOUS BLUEBERRY MUFFINS

1 cup unbleached flour
¾ cup whole wheat flour
¼ cup wheat germ
4 teaspoons baking powder
½ teaspoon cream of tartar
1 teaspoon salt
1 large egg
½ teaspoon vanilla
6 tablespoons cold pressed oil
¼ cup raw sugar
1 tablespoon lecithin (available at a health food store)
1 cup milk
2/3 cup fresh blueberries

Blend dry ingredients. Beat egg, vanilla, oil, sugar and lecithin together and add to the dry ingredients. Add milk all at once. Stir until mixed, but lumpy. Fold in blueberries. Fill greased muffin tins 2/3 full. Bake at 375° for 20 to 25 minutes. Makes 12 muffins.

BRAN MUFFINS

2 cups yogurt
1 egg
¼ cup sorghum
4 tablespoons molasses
2 tablespoons clarified butter
2 cups whole wheat flour
1½ cups whole bran
¾ teaspoon salt
1¼ teaspoons baking soda
1 cup seedless raisins

Combine yogurt, egg, sorghum, molasses and butter, mixing well. Add dry ingredients and then the raisins. (Do not over-mix.) Pour into oiled muffin tin and bake at 425° for about 15 to 20 minutes. Makes about 2 dozen muffins.

Variations:

If a lighter muffin is desired use half whole wheat flour and half unbleached white flour.

For a nuttier taste, decrease bran to ¾ cup and add ¾ cup wheat germ.

HEALTH FOOD STORE MUFFINS

¼ cup sesame oil
¾ cup milk
2 to 3 tablespoons sorghum
¼ cup raw or brown sugar
1 egg
1¼ teaspoons baking powder
¼ teaspoon salt
½ cup whole wheat flour
3/8 cup wheat germ
2 tablespoons rolled oats
2 tablespoons soy flour
¼ cup powdered dry milk
¼ cup brewer's yeast
¼ cup sunflower seeds
¼ cup sesame seeds (hulled)
½ cup seedless raisins
½ cup chopped nuts

Combine oil, milk, sorghum, sugar and egg. Mix all dry ingredients together. Pour liquid into dry ingredients and stir well, but do not over-mix. Pour into a buttered muffin tin and bake for 18 minutes at 375º. Serves 12-15.

CAROB MUFFINS

2½ cups whole wheat flour
1 cup millet flour
1 tablespoon baking powder
1½ teaspoons salt
½ cup carob powder
1 cup raw sugar
4 beaten eggs
2 to 3 cups milk

Mix dry ingredients; combine eggs and milk and add to the dry mixture. Stir until batter is a creamy consistency. Pour into muffin tin and bake at 375° until a toothpick comes out clean. (About 20 to 30 minutes.) Makes 12 muffins.

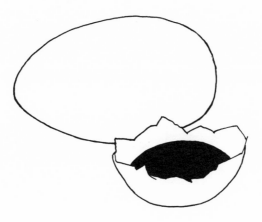

CARROT BREAD

1 package dry yeast
1/3 cup lukewarm water
1 cup oat flour
½ cup potato starch
1/3 cup soy flour
3 tablespoons skim milk powder
½ teaspoon salt
1½ teaspoons cinnamon
¼ teaspoon nutmeg
2 eggs
½ cup date sugar or natural sweetener
2/3 cup cold-pressed oil
2 cups shredded raw carrots
¾ cup coarsely chopped nuts

Oil a 9 x 2½ x 4½ inch loaf pan. Dissolve dry yeast in warm water; set aside. Sift dry ingredients together except the date sugar.

In a mixing bowl, beat eggs lightly; gradually add date sugar. Stir in oil. Gradually stir in sifted dry ingredients and blend until well combined. Stir in shredded, raw carrots and nuts. Slowly add the yeast mixture and blend.

Pour batter into pan and allow to rest in warm place for 20 minutes. Bake in a preheated 350° oven for 1 hour and 15 minutes. Cool for 10 minutes and remove from pan. Makes 1 loaf.

RICE FLOUR LOAF

1 cup rice flour
½ cup sunflower seeds
½ cup sesame seeds
½ teaspoon salt
1 tablespoon finely chopped fresh parsley
1 medium-size onion, finely chopped
1 medium-size carrot, grated
2 eggs, separated
2 tablespoons clarified butter or oil
¾ cup soy milk or milk
¼ cup grated cheese
3 tablespoons protein powder (optional)

Make sunflower and sesame meal by grinding the seeds in a blender, seed grinder or coffee mill.

Place all ingredients, except the egg whites, in a bowl and mix well. In another bowl, beat egg whites until stiff and almost dry and then fold into the batter.

Pour batter into an oiled and floured 9 x 5 x 3 inch loaf pan and sprinkle the top with sesame seeds, if desired. Bake at 350° for 50 to 60 minutes or until a knife inserted in the center comes out clean. Makes 1 loaf.

RYE BREAD

2 cups warm water (105°)
2 packages active dry yeast
1 tablespoon salt
¼ cup dark molasses
2 tablespoons butter, softened
1 to 2 tablespoons caraway seed, to taste
3 cups unsifted rye flour
3 cups unsifted whole wheat flour
cornmeal
1 egg white, slightly beaten
extra caraway seeds

Sprinkle yeast over warm water in a large bowl, stirring until dissolved. Add salt, molasses, butter, caraway seed, rye flour and 1½ cups of the wheat flour. Beat with a wooden spoon until smooth—about 2 minutes.

Gradually add the rest of the wheat flour; mix in with hands until dough leaves the sides of the bowl.

Turn dough onto a lightly floured board. (Dough will be stiff.) Knead until smooth—about 10 minutes. Place in a lightly greased, large bowl; turn to bring the greased side up. Cover with a towel; let rise until double in bulk—about 1 hour.

Grease a large cookie sheet; sprinkle with cornmeal. Punch down dough. Turn out unto lightly floured pastry cloth. Divide in half. Make two oval loaves. Place them 3 inches apart on the cookie sheet. With a sharp knife, cut 5 slashes diagonally across each loaf.

Cover with a towel. Let rise until double—about 1 hour. Preheat oven to 375°. Bake bread for 40 to 50 minutes or until loaf sounds hollow when rapped with knuckle. Remove to a wire rack. Brush tops of loaves with egg white; sprinkle with caraway seed; cool. Makes 2 loaves.

HIGH PROTEIN BREAD

1 cup whole wheat flour
1 cup soy flour
1 cup wheat germ
2/3 cup protein powder (available from health food
   store)
4 teaspoons baking powder
1 teaspoon salt
1 teaspoon cinnamon
¼ teaspoon nutmeg
¼ teaspoon allspice
¼ teaspoon ginger
2 eggs
¼ cup clarified butter or oil
½ cup sorghum
1 cup yogurt or sour cream
1 teaspoon vanilla
1 cup chopped walnuts
½ cup chopped pecans
½ cup chopped cashews

Mix together all the dry ingredients. Combine eggs,
butter, sorghum, yogurt and vanilla. Beat well and add to
the dry ingredients. Stir in the nuts. Pour into 2 well-greased
9 x 5 x 3 inch loaf pans and bake at 350° for 45 to 60
minutes. Makes 2 loaves.

CHALLAH

5 cups unsifted, unbleached flour
2 tablespoons raw sugar
1½ teaspoons salt
1 package active dry yeast
1/3 cup butter
pinch of powdered saffron
1 cup hot water (120°)
4 eggs
1 teaspoon cold water
¼ teaspoon poppy seeds

Combine 1¼ cups of the flour with sugar, salt and yeast. Add butter. Dissolve saffron in water. Add to dry ingredients and beat for 2 minutes. Add 3 of the eggs, 1 egg white and ½ cup more flour. Beat at high speed for 2 minutes. Stir in additional flour to make a soft dough. Turn onto a floured board; knead about 8 to 10 minutes. Place in a greased bowl; turn to grease top of dough. Cover; let rise in warm place until doubled—about 1 hour.

Punch down; turn onto floured board. Divide in half. Then divide each half into 2 pieces, one about 1/3, the other about 2/3 of the dough. Form each large piece into three 12 inch ropes. Braid ropes; pinch ends. Shape each smaller piece into three 10 inch ropes. Braid; place on top of the large braids. Seal braids together at ends. Place on greased baking sheets.

Brush egg yolk mixed with cold water on the loaves. Sprinkle with poppy seeds. Let rise, uncovered, until double—about 1 hour. Bake at 400° for 20 to 25 minutes. Makes 2 loaves.

HUSH PUPPIES

2 cups corn meal
1 cup whole wheat flour
1 teaspoon baking powder
½ teaspoon baking soda
1 teaspoon salt
½ teaspoon raw sugar
½ cup chopped onions
½ cup buttermilk
¾ cup water
½ cup melted butter
1 egg

Sift together corn meal, flour, baking powder, soda, salt and sugar in a bowl. Add onions, buttermilk and water. Mix well. Add butter and egg and blend. Drop by small tablespoons into preheated clarified butter or oil (370°). Cook until golden brown. Makes about 30.

SPOON BREAD

1 cup yellow corn meal
1 cup cold water
1 cup boiling water
2 tablespoons butter
3 eggs
1½ cups milk
1 teaspoon salt
2 tablespoons wheat germ

In a saucepan, stir corn meal and cold water until smooth. Then add the boiling water and cook until thickened. Remove from heat and stir in butter, eggs, milk, salt and wheat germ. Mix well and pour into well-buttered 8 x 8 inch baking dish.

Bake at 375° for 50 minutes. Serve hot. Makes 4-6 servings.

Desserts

BANANAS HAWAIIAN

¾ cup fresh flaked coconut
3 tablespoons butter
½ cup firmly packed brown sugar
½ teaspoon vanilla
¼ teaspoon ground cinnamon
1/3 cup water
6 bananas, peeled and sliced

Heat coconut in large skillet until toasted. Stir to brown evenly. Remove to a sheet of foil to cool.

Add butter, sugar, vanilla, cinnamon and water to the skillet. Heat until bubbly. Add bananas and cook until slices are heated through. Add toasted coconut and stir to coat the bananas.

Serve in small dishes as dessert. Also delicious spooned over ice cream. Serves 6.

Variation:

Eliminate brown sugar and use ¼ - 1/3 cup pure maple syrup. Decrease water to 2 tablespoons.

CAROB BROWNIES

2/3 cup whole wheat flour
½ teaspoon baking powder
¼ teaspoon salt
4 tablespoons carob powder
1/3 cup butter, melted
2 eggs, well beaten
1 cup brown sugar
½ cup chopped walnuts
1 teaspoon vanilla

Combine flour, baking powder and salt. Sift twice; set aside. Add carob powder to the melted butter. Beat eggs; gradually add sugar, beating thoroughly. Add the carob mixture to the egg mixture. Blend in the flour and mix well. Mix in nuts and vanilla.

Spread in a buttered pan. Bake at 350° for about 25 minutes. Cut into squares. Makes about 16 brownies.

Variation:
Use soy flour instead of whole wheat flour.
Use hulled sunflower seeds in place of the walnuts.

CAROB FUDGE

½ cup raisins, soaked
½ cup ground nuts (cashews and almonds)
1 teaspoon vanilla
1 tablespoon liquid lecithin (available at health food stores)
2/3 cup butter, softened
2/3 cup carob powder
2/3 cup soy powder
½ cup chopped nuts (pecans or walnuts)

In blender, mix raisins, ground nuts, vanilla, lecithin and a little butter until smooth. Transfer to a mixing bowl and add the rest of the butter.

Dry roast carob powder in a wok until it smells cooked (3 to 5 minutes on medium heat). Stir in the soy powder and remove from heat. Sift carob and soy into the ingredients in the bowl; stir to combine well.

Spread on a tray and freeze for a few hours. Cut into pieces and serve immediately. Makes about 12 pieces.

CAROB BANANA PUDDING

10 bananas, peeled and mashed
5 eggs, beaten
2 cups milk
1 teaspoon vanilla
½ cup carob powder

Combine the first 4 ingredients, sift carob powder into the mixture a little at a time until well blended. Pour into a buttered casserole or 9 x 13 inch baking pan; bake at 350° for 30 to 45 minutes or until firm. Serves 6-8.

KITCHEN SINK COOKIES

1 cup whole wheat flour
¼ cup soy flour
1 1/3 cups rolled oats
¾ cup unsweetened flaked coconut
¼ cup milk powder
½ teaspoon salt
1 teaspoon cinnamon
½ teaspoon powdered ginger
2/3 cup chopped dates
2/3 cup carob chips
¼ cup chopped cashews
1/3 cup sunflower seeds
2 eggs, beaten
¼ cup clarified butter or oil
¼ cup molasses
¼ cup raw sugar

Stir together all of the dry ingredients into a large bowl. Beat the eggs in a small bowl; add the butter and then molasses, beating thoroughly. Pour the liquid mixture into the dry ingredients and combine until evenly moistened. (If the mixture seems too dry, add milk or water until the dough is of drop cookie consistency.)

Drop by the teaspoonful onto an ungreased cookie sheet and bake at 350° for 10 to 12 minutes. Makes 4 dozen.

OATMEAL COOKIES

1 cup raisins
1 cup unbleached flour
1 cup whole wheat flour
½ teaspoon salt
½ teaspoon soda
1½ teaspoon cinnamon
½ teaspoon allspice
½ teaspoon cloves
1 cup butter
½ cup sorghum
2 eggs
2 cups old fashioned oats
1 teaspoon vanilla
½ cup chopped walnuts

Put raisins in saucepan, cover with water, and boil the water away, being careful not to let the raisins burn. Mix dry ingredients; set aside.

Beat together butter and sorghum until light and fluffy. Add eggs. Slowly add oats and then dry ingredients. Stir in vanilla, raisins and nuts. (If mixture is very thick, add 1 or 2 tablespoons of water.)

Drop by the teaspoon on ungreased cookie sheet. Bake at 350° for 12 to 15 minutes until golden brown. Makes 6 dozen.

WHEAT GERM ORANGE COOKIES

¼ cup rice syrup or sorghum
2 tablespoons raw sugar
½ cup clarified butter or oil
¼ cup fresh orange juice
2 teaspoons baking powder
1 teaspoon vanilla
1 cup wheat germ
1¾ cups graham flour
½ cup milk

Blend all ingredients together thoroughly and drop by the tablespoonful onto greased cookie sheet. Bake at 350° for 8 to 10 minutes or until brown. Makes about 4 dozen cookies.

SPEECY SPICEY COOKIES

½ cup clarified butter
1/3 cup maple syrup
1 cup whole wheat flour
1 cup unbleached white flour
½ teaspoon salt
1 teaspoon baking powder
½ teaspoon baking soda
1½ teaspoons ginger
1½ teaspoons allspice
¼ teaspoon nutmeg
1 egg
¼ cup water

Sift dry ingredients together into a mixing bowl. Melt clarified butter in a saucepan over low heat. Stir in syrup and cool. Mix egg with butter and syrup, then add to the dry ingredients. Mix and beat until smooth. (You may need to add a bit more water.) Chill for 2 to 3 hours.

Heat oven to 350°. Lightly oil 2 cookie sheets. Roll dough to desired thickness and cut with a cookie cutter. Bake for 15 to 20 minutes. Makes about 3 to 4 dozen.

DUTCH BUTTER COOKIES

1 cup butter
1/3 cup pure maple syrup
1 egg, separated
1 teaspoon vanilla
2½ cups unbleached flour
1 cup finely ground walnuts

Cream butter and syrup; add egg yolk and vanilla, then flour.

Pat very thin on 2 lightly buttered cookie sheets. Brush with unbeaten egg white, then sprinkle with nuts. Bake for 45 minutes at 250°. Cut in squares and remove from cookie sheet immediately. Makes about 3 to 4 dozen cookies, depending on the size of squares cut.

CHEESE COOKIES

1 cup butter
1 cup ricotta cheese
1 cup unbleached flour
1 cup whole wheat flour
12 ounce box of raisins

Cream together butter and cheese. Add flour and mix well. Wrap in waxed paper and place in refrigerator to cool.

Put raisins in a saucepan and cover them with water. Boil down until there is no water left in the pan, being careful not to scorch the raisins. Grind raisins in food grinder or blender.

Roll the dough into thin sheets and cut into 3 inch squares. Place a teaspoon of the ground raisins in the center of each square and fold into a triangle. Place on a lightly greased cookie sheet and bake at 350° for 25 minutes. Makes about 4 dozen cookies.

FRUIT SANDWICHES

¾ cup molasses or sorghum
¾ cup clarified butter
2 cups whole wheat flour
1¾ cups rolled oats
¼ cup wheat germ
1 cup chopped dried apricots
½ cup chopped prunes
½ cup seedless raisins
½ cup dates
1 tablespoon cornstarch or arrowroot
½ cup whey or water
2 tablespoons lemon juice
1 cup chopped walnuts or pecans

Mix molasses, butter, flour, oats and wheat germ. Pour half of this mixture into a buttered 8 x 12 inch baking pan.

Put apricots, prunes, raisins, dates, cornstarch, whey and lemon juice in a saucepan. Cook over low heat, stirring constantly, until mixture thickens and blends together. Cool and pour over crumb mixture in baking dish.

Pour the remaining crumb mixture over the top of the fruit. Sprinkle nuts over the top.

Bake in a hot (400°) oven for about 25 minutes. Cool slightly and then cut into bars. Makes about 8 bars.

SOFT BRAN COOKIES

¼ cup butter
½ cup sorghum
2 eggs
1 cup bran
1 teaspoon vanilla
½ cup soy grits
2/3 cup rye flour
1 1/3 cup unbleached flour
2 teaspoons baking powder
¾ to 1 cup milk

Mix butter and sorghum; add beaten eggs. Add bran and vanilla and mix well. Stir in grits, flour and baking powder. Add milk slowly and stir until smooth.

Spoon onto greased cookie sheet. Bake at 400° for about 10 minutes. Makes 24 large cookies.

COCONUT WHEAT GERM BARS

¼ cup rice syrup or sorghum
2 tablespoons raw sugar
1/3 cup clarified butter or oil
3 eggs, beaten
2 teaspoons lemon extract
1 cup wheat germ
2 cups unsweetened, dried flaked coconut
1 cup raisins, steamed

Thoroughly blend together the rice syrup, sugar, butter, eggs and lemon extract. Add to this mixture the wheat germ, coconut and raisins. Mix thoroughly.

Pour the dough into a greased 12 x 8 x 2 inch pan. Bake at 325° for 25 to 30 minutes. Cut into 1 x 4 inch bars while still warm. Makes 2 dozen bars.

SHEERA

6 or 7 cardamom pods
2 cups milk
¾ cup raw sugar or fructose
¾ cup melted butter
1 cup farina or cream-of-rice cereal
¼ cup chopped raw cashews
¼ cup raisins

Begin by breaking open the cardamom pods and gathering the small seeds inside. Discard the outer shells and crush the seeds; set aside. In a saucepan, heat the milk and sugar, stirring occasionally until scalding, not quite boiling; set aside.

In a large saucepan, combine butter and farina, stirring over a medium heat about 5 minutes. Add the chopped cashews and continue to cook until the cereal turns a tawny color. Add the hot milk mixture, being careful, as it will spatter. Add the raisins and continue stirring until the sheera thickens and starts to draw away from the sides of the pan.

Add the crushed cardamom seeds and turn out on a lightly buttered serving dish. Sheera can be served warm or cut into squares when cooled. Serves 12.

ALMOND CREAM

1 quart half and half
1 1/3 cups powdered milk
1/8 teaspoon ground cardamom
2 tablespoons quick-mixing gravy flour
2 egg yolks
3 tablespoons pure maple syrup
½ teaspoon almond extract
2 ounces finely ground almonds (about 1 cup)

In a saucepan, beat half and half with powdered milk until smooth. Bring to a boil, stirring to prevent sticking. Simmer for 5 to 10 minutes and then add cardamom. Add flour by sprinkling over the surface as you beat the mixture. Make sure there are no lumps. Cook for another 10 minutes to thicken.

In a bowl, combine egg yolks, syrup and almond extract. Add some of the milk mixture to the eggs and stir well until the egg is well diffused. Then add the egg mixture to the saucepan. Add almonds and bring to a boil again. Mixture should be thickened now.

Remove from heat, cover, and refrigerate for about 3 hours. Serve in small dessert cups, topped with a dollop of whipped cream and a slivered almond. (This dessert is very rich, thus the small servings.) Can serve 6.

FROZEN PAPAYA CREAM

2 fresh, ripe papayas
4 tablespoons fresh lime juice
1/3 cup light honey
½ cup heavy cream
lime wedges

Cut papayas in half lengthwise; remove and discard the seeds. Scoop out 4 small balls with a melon baller, reserving for garnish. Carefully scoop out remaining pulp, reserving papaya shells. Puree papaya with lime juice and honey in blender until smooth.

Beat the cream until stiff. Quickly but gently fold papaya into cream. Pour mixture into a shallow 8 inch cake pan. Place in freezer for 1 hour or until frozen about 1 inch around the edge of the pan. Stir with a spoon. Return to freezer for another 30 minutes to 1 hour or until soft-frozen.

Spoon mixture into reserved papaya shells. Garnish with a wedge of lime and reserved papaya balls. Return to freezer for a few minutes until ready to serve. Serves 4.

BAKED RICE CUSTARD

3 cups milk, scalded
1½ cups cooked rice (brown or basmati)
1 tablespoon butter
3 eggs, beaten
½ cup raw sugar
½ teaspoon nutmeg
½ teaspoon vanilla
1/3 cup raisins

Pour hot milk into rice and butter and stir until smooth. Add other ingredients and mix well.

Bake in buttered baking dish at 325° about 35 to 40 minutes, until custard is done (silver knife inserted in the middle of custard comes out clean). Serves 6.

MILLET RICE PUDDING

1½ cups cooked rice
1 cup cooked millet
2 eggs
¼ to ½ cup raw sugar
½ cup yogurt
¼ cup papaya syrup or fresh orange juice
½ cup sliced dates or raisins
1 teaspoon vanilla
¼ cup unsweetened shredded coconut

Combine all ingredients except the coconut. Pour into a buttered 1½ quart baking dish and sprinkle the coconut on top.

Bake for 45 minutes at 375°. Serves 6.

MOTHER'S APPLE CAKE

½ pound butter, softened
1½ cups raw sugar
2 eggs
2 cups unbleached or whole wheat flour
½ teaspoon baking soda
2 teaspoons baking powder
1 cup raisins
2 teaspoons cinnamon
½ teaspoon nutmeg
1 cup chopped walnuts
4 cups raw apple, peeled and cubed

Cream sugar into butter, stir in eggs and then add flour and rest of ingredients. Bake at 350° in buttered 12 x 16 inch pan about 35 minutes. Serves 24.

Variations:
Omit raw sugar and use 1 cup fructose and ½ cup sorghum.
In place of the raisins use fresh shredded coconut.

APPLE CRISP

1 cup whole wheat flour
1 cup oats
½ teaspoon salt
½ teaspoon baking soda
½ cup butter
¼ cup pure maple syrup
8 apples, peeled, cored and sliced
2 teaspoons cinnamon

Preheat oven to 350°. Mix together flour, oats, salt and soda. Cut butter and syrup into the dry ingredients with 2 knives or a pastry blender until small, uniform balls are formed.

Place apples in the bottom of a buttered 9 x 9 inch pan; sprinkle with cinnamon. Cover with oat mixture and bake for 50 minutes, or until done. Makes 6 servings.

Variation:
Use half apples and half pears; or, in addition to apples, add ½ cup fresh blueberries or strawberries.

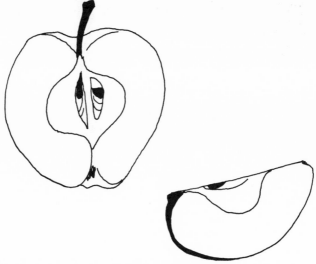

APPLE-PEACH TORTE

2 cups peeled and sliced apples
2 cups peeled and sliced peaches, ripe but firm
1/3 cup pure maple syrup
½ teaspoon cinnamon
½ cup butter
1/3 cup raw sugar
½ teaspoon vanilla
1 cup unbleached flour
8 ounces cream cheese
¼ cup raw sugar
1 egg
¼ teaspoon vanilla

Place apples in a large bowl. Combine syrup and cinnamon and pour over apples. Set aside.

Cream butter and 1/3 of sugar until light and fluffy. Add vanilla. Blend well. Add flour and mix well. Form into a ball. With fingers, press dough in the bottom and sides of a 10 inch spring form pan.

Mix cream cheese and 1/4 cup sugar. Add egg and vanilla and beat until smooth and creamy. Pour mixture into pastry in pan. Sprinkle apples on top of the cheese mixture. Bake at 450° for 10 minutes. Reduce oven temperature to 400° and continue baking for 25 to 30 minutes. Loosen rim of pan while cooling. Delicious served warm. Serves 6.

MOM'S CARROT CAKE

3 cups unbleached flour
2 cups raw sugar
2 teaspoons baking powder
2 teaspoons baking soda
1 teaspoon cinnamon
½ teaspoon salt
1½ cups clarified butter or oil, or combination of
    both
4 egg yolks
3 cups grated carrots
½ cup coarsely chopped walnuts
4 egg whites

Sift together the flour, sugar, baking powder, soda, cinnamon and salt. Mix well and add butter, egg yolks, grated carrot and nuts. Beat egg whites until stiff. Fold into the cake mixture.

Bake in a spring tube pan at 325° for 55 minutes. Then turn oven to 350° and bake for another 15 minutes. Serves 12.

CAROB CARROT CAKE

1½ cups unbleached flour
1½ cups whole wheat flour
1 cup raw sugar or brown sugar
2 teaspoons baking powder
2 teaspoons baking soda
6 tablespoons carob powder
1½ teaspoons cinnamon
½ teaspoon salt
1 cup clarified butter
½ cup packed tofu
4 eggs
2 cups grated carrots
½ cup coarsely chopped walnuts
½ cup sorghum
½ cup maple syrup

Sift together flour, sugar, baking powder, soda, carob powder, cinnamon and salt. Blend in blender the butter, tofu, eggs, grated carrots and nuts. Add to dry ingredients along with sorghum and maple syrup; stir until well blended.

Bake in a bundt pan at 325° for 55 minutes. Increase heat to 350° and bake for another 15 minutes. Makes about 12 servings.

NO-SUGAR CARROT CAKE

1¼ cups whole wheat flour
1½ teaspoon baking powder
1 teaspoon salt
2 teaspoons cinnamon
2/3 cup pure maple syrup
¾ cup clarified butter or oil
2 eggs
2 teaspoons vanilla
½ cup raisins
1 cup grated carrots
1 cup chopped walnuts or pecans

Combine dry ingredients. Add syrup and other liquids. Beat at low speed for 1 minute, then beat 2 minutes at medium speed. Add raisins, carrots and nuts.

Pour into a 9 x 9 inch greased pan or a small greased and floured bundt pan. Bake in a 350° oven for 35 to 45 minutes. Makes 10 to 12 slices.

CARROT-HAZELNUT CAKE

2 cups raw sugar
1½ cups clarified butter or oil
4 eggs
2¼ cups flour
2 teaspoons salt
2 teaspoons baking soda
2 teaspoons cinnamon
3 cups grated carrots
1½ cups coarsely chopped hazelnuts

Cream sugar, oil and eggs. Add flour, salt, soda and cinnamon alternately with carrots. Mix in nuts. Pour into a greased and floured 8 x 12 inch pan and bake at 300° for 1 hour. Frost with Cream Cheese Frosting.

CREAM CHEESE FROSTING

8 ounces cream cheese
¼ cup butter
2 teaspoons vanilla
1 cup light honey

Combine ingredients and beat until creamy. Frost cake and, if necessary, place in refrigerator until served.

CREAMY CHEESECAKE

1/3 cup unsalted butter
1/3 cup toasted coconut
1/3 cup wheat germ
3 to 4 whole graham crackers, crushed
1 tablespoon raw sugar
1 teaspoon molasses
½ teaspoon cinnamon
1 egg, plus 3 yolks
1 cup small-curd cottage cheese
2/3 cup sour cream
4 tablespoons rice syrup
5 tablespoons date sugar or fructose
2 teaspoons vanilla extract

Melt the butter in a small pan. Add coconut, wheat germ, graham crackers, raw sugar, molasses and cinnamon. Stir well. Put the mixture into an 8 or 9 inch pie pan.

In a large mixing bowl, beat eggs. Add cottage cheese and sour cream; blend well. Add rice syrup, date sugar and vanilla; blend again. Pour into crust. Bake in preheated oven, at 350° for 35 minutes or until done. Sprinkle with chopped nuts or dates. Chill before serving. Serves 8.

COTTAGE CHEESE CHEESECAKE

16 ounces dry cottage cheese
8 ounces kefir cheese or cream cheese
1 cup dairy sour cream
3 large eggs
7/8 cup raw sugar
1 teaspoon vanilla
1 tablespoon cornstarch
¼ cup lemon juice
grated rind from 1 lemon
2 to 3 tablespoons wheat germ

Combine all ingredients except wheat germ in a blender until smooth. Generously butter a deep pie dish, sprinkle with wheat germ, and pour in filling. Bake at 350° for about 1 hour. Let cool before cutting. Serves 10.

Variation:
    Omit sour cream and add 1 cup of pineapple yogurt.

NUTTY CHEESECAKE

1 cup raw cashews
2/3 cup wheat germ
2/3 cup whole wheat flour
½ teaspoon ground cinnamon
1/8 teaspoon ground allspice
1/8 teaspoon ground nutmeg
3 tablespoons butter
1½ teaspoon raw sugar
3 eggs
1¼ cups dairy sour cream
8 ounces cream cheese
½ cup rice syrup or sorghum or sugar
2 tablespoons frozen orange juice concentrate
½ teaspoon vanilla
¼ teaspoon ground allspice
¼ teaspoon ground cinnamon
¼ teaspoon ground nutmeg
2 tablespoons light cream or milk

Place cashews in blender; cover; whirl until fine. (You will have 2/3 cup.) Place in a medium-size bowl; add wheat germ, flour, cinnamon, allspice, nutmeg, butter and sugar. Work in with fingers until mixture is crumbly. Press into a 9 inch pie plate to form a shell.

Wash and dry blender container. Blend together until smooth eggs, sour cream, ½ of the cream cheese, rice syrup, orange juice concentrate, vanilla, allspice, cinnamon and nutmeg. Slowly pour into the prepared pie shell.

Bake in a slow oven (250°) for 1 hour. The cheesecake should be golden, but not brown.

Refrigerate within 5 to 10 minutes after removing from oven. Chill overnight.

Whip remaining half of cream cheese with 2 table-spoons cream. Garnish pie with whipped cream cheese and decorate with slivers of orange rind, if you wish. Serves 6.

SPICY YOGURT CAKE

½ cup butter
1½ cups raw sugar
3 eggs
2 cups sifted unbleached flour
1 teaspoon baking powder
1 teaspoon baking soda
¼ teaspoon salt
½ teaspoon ground nutmeg
1 teaspoon ground cinnamon
¼ teaspoon ground cloves
1 cup yogurt
½ teaspoon vanilla

Grease a 13 x 9 x 2 inch baking pan. Dust with flour. Beat butter and sugar in a large bowl. Add eggs, one at a time, beating well after each. Sift together flour, baking powder, soda, salt, nutmeg, cinnamon and cloves; stir into creamed mixture alternately with yogurt, just until blended. Stir in vanilla. Pour into pan. Bake in moderate (350°) oven for 35 to 45 minutes. Frost with Broiled Coconut Frosting.

BROILED COCONUT FROSTING

¾ cup shredded coconut
1/3 cup finely chopped walnuts
½ cup firmly packed brown sugar
2 tablespoons melted butter
¼ cup heavy cream
¼ teaspoon vanilla

Combine coconut, walnuts, sugar and butter in a small bowl. Stir in cream and vanilla. Blend thoroughly. Spread evenly over cake. Place cake under broiler with top about 5 inches from heat. Broil 3 to 5 minutes until frosting is lightly browned and bubbly. Cake makes about 15 servings.

GINGERBREAD

½ cup raw sugar
¼ pound butter, softened
1 large egg
1 cup molasses
1 cup hot water
2 cups unbleached or whole wheat flour
½ cup wheat germ
1½ teaspoons baking soda
1 teaspoon cinnamon
1 teaspoon ginger
½ teaspoon cloves
3/8 teaspoon salt
1 cup raisins

Cream sugar into the softened butter. Add egg, molasses and hot water. Stir in dry ingredients, including raisins.

Bake in a buttered 9 x 13 inch pan at 350° for 35 to 40 minutes or until gingerbread begins to draw away from sides of the pan. Serve with fresh whipped cream or creamed topping (recipe follows), if desired. Makes about 8 servings.

CREAMED TOPPING

3 ounces cream cheese
½ cup sour cream
1 cup heavy cream

Whip the ingredients together until smooth and creamy.

NO-SUGAR CAKE

2 very ripe bananas, mashed
1 cup chopped dates
1 cup buttermilk or sour milk
2/3 cup butter
3 eggs, separated
1 cup rice syrup
2½ cups whole wheat pastry flour
1 teaspoon baking powder
1 teaspoon salt
¾ teaspoon baking soda

Place banana, ½ cup chopped dates and milk in blender and puree; set aside. In a mixing bowl cream butter, egg yolks and rice syrup. Sift together flour, baking powder, salt and soda and add to the eggs. Mix at medium speed for 2 to 3 minutes. Add the banana mixture and mix well.

Beat egg whites until stiff but not dry and fold into the batter.

Pour into three 8 inch oiled and floured cake pans. Bake at 350° for 25 to 30 minutes. Frost with Mocha Cream Frosting.

MOCHA CREAM FROSTING

¼ cup carob powder
3 tablespoons honey or fructose or maple syrup
2 to 3 teaspoons ground malt or instant coffee
1/8 teaspoon salt
2 cups heavy cream

To the dry ingredients, add a little cream and mix until smooth. Add remaining cream and whip.

195

STUFFED BAKED APPLES

6 medium-size cooking apples
12 pitted dates
3 tablespoons finely chopped walnuts
1 teaspoon cinnamon
½ teaspoon nutmeg
½ teaspoon allspice
6 teaspoons butter
½ cup maple syrup

Core apples. Cut dates into pieces, mix with walnuts and spices, and place in each apple. Top each with 1 teaspoon butter.

Place apples in a baking pan to which ¼ inch of water has been added. Pour maple syrup over apples. Bake in moderate oven for 45 minutes. Baste occasionally during baking with the syrup in the pan, adding more if necessary. Serve warm, with whipped cream or special topping (recipe p. 194) if desired. Serves 6.

PUMPKIN CUSTARD

1 cup pumpkin
1 egg
½ cup molasses
½ teaspoon salt
½ teaspoon cinnamon
¼ teaspoon nutmeg
¼ teaspoon cloves
1 cup heavy cream

Blend pumpkin, egg, molasses, salt and spices together with electric mixer. Gradually add cream. Beat well, then pour into four custard cups. Set cups in a shallow pan of hot water and bake at 325° for 40 minutes, or until done. Serves 4.

WHIPPED APRICOTS

2 cups dried apricots
1 cup heavy cream
1 teaspoon vanilla
½ cup shredded coconut

Place apricots in a saucepan, add ½ cup water, cover and steam until all water has evaporated and apricots are soft. Put apricots in blender and puree.
Beat cream until stiff. Add vanilla and beat again. Fold apricots and coconut into whipped cream until well blended. Serve in small bowls. Makes about 4-6 servings.

EGGLESS PUMPKIN PIE

cooked pie crust (recipe p. 16)
8 tablespoons light honey
½ teaspoon salt
1¼ teaspoon cinnamon
½ teaspoon ginger
½ teaspoon nutmeg
¼ teaspoon cloves
2 tablespoons molasses
2 tablespoons agar, dissolved over low heat
1½ cups cooked pumpkin, well mashed
1½ cups yogurt

Mix all the above ingredients until smooth and creamy. Slowly pour into a baked pie crust and chill in the refrigerator. It will "set up" nicely as it cools. Serves about 8.

Beverages

MINT JULIP

½ cup grape juice
3 cups pineapple juice
2 cups fresh orange juice
2 teaspoons lemon juice
½ cup crushed mint leaves

Pour grape, pineapple, orange and lemon juices into a pitcher containing mint leaves. Stir and serve in pre-chilled glasses. Garnish with a few mint sprigs. Serves 4-6.

MINT FRESHENER

12 sprigs fresh mint, crushed
1½ quarts boiling water
juice of 2 lemons
juice of 4 oranges
honey to taste

Place mint in a heavy dish and pour boiling water over; steep for 15 to 30 minutes. Strain and chill. Add orange juice, lemon juice and sweetener. Pour over crushed ice in tall glasses. Garnish with fresh mint leaves. Serves 6-8.

MINT LEMONADE

4 lemons
1 lime
5 cups water
honey or sugar to taste
mint cubes (recipe follows)

Squeeze lemons and lime. Add water to juice in a large pitcher. Sweeten to taste. Pour lemonade over mint ice cubes in a tall glass. Serves 4.

MINT ICE CUBES

2 cups freshly picked mint
2 cups water
3 tablespoons sugar or honey (optional)

Crush mint leaves with a potato masher. Put mint in a pan and cover with water. Bring mixture to boil. When boiling, turn down heat to simmer and cover pan with an inverted pan lid filled with ice cubes.* Remove pan from heat and allow to steep for 10 minutes. Strain. If desired, add sweetener and stir well to dissolve. Pour mixture into ice cube trays and freeze. Makes about 24 ice cubes.

* Ice cubes in the inverted lid cool the rising steam in the pan, causing it to condense and fall back so no flavor is lost. All the ice and water in the lid is discarded.

MANGO MILKSHAKE

1 large, fresh, ripe mango
3 cups cold milk
2 tablespoons light honey
ground cinnamon

Peel mango carefully over a bowl so as to catch all the juice. Cut away the pulp from the large seed and discard the seed. Crush the mango with a potato masher and remove any stringy fibers. Place 1 cup of the mango pulp in a blender; add milk and honey and blend until smooth. Adjust taste, as desired, by adding more mango or honey. Pour into tall glasses and sprinkle with ground cinnamon. Serves 3.

Variation:
½ cup of fresh strawberries or other summer fruit may be added to the blender with the milk and honey.

MASALA TEA

Handful of fresh, green mint leaves
4 cups water
pinch of garam masala spices (from Indian food store)
Darjeeling black tea

Boil mint in water; add a pinch of the masala mixture and turn off heat. Add about 1 teaspoon tea and cover the pot, allowing the tea to brew for about 2 to 3 minutes. Serve with or without cream and honey. Makes 4 cups.

Note: If garam masala is not available, add dashes of cinnamon, mace, ginger, cayenne and coriander.

COFFEE SUBSTITUTE

1 pound barley
¼ pound chicory
whipped cream
cinnamon

Roast barley on a large flat pan in a 400° oven until nicely brown. Mix with the chicory. Use desired amount and perk in a coffee pot until a fragrant brew with a pleasing, dark brown color is produced.
Serve with a little honey, a dollop of whipped cream and a dash of cinnamon.

YOGURT DRINK

2 cups yogurt
1 cup water
1 tablespoon lime juice
honey to taste
crushed ice
1 teaspoon ground pistachios

Blend yogurt with water and lime juice. Add honey to taste and pour over crushed ice in a tall glass. Top with ground nuts. Serves 2.

Variations:
Use papaya concentrate instead of the honey; use 1 to 2 teaspoons rose water instead of the lime juice.

A salty yogurt drink can be made by eliminating the honey and adding ½ teaspoon salt and ½ teaspoon roasted ground cumin seed with a pinch of cayenne to the drink.

ALMOND MILK

1 cup almonds
4 cups water
4 black peppercorns
½ cup raw sugar or other sweetener

Blanch the almonds. Put almonds, water and pepper-corns in a blender and blend well at high speed. Strain through muslin into a pitcher and add the sweetener. Chill well and serve. Serves 4.

ANISE MILK

¼ cup pistachio nuts
¼ cup almonds
1 cup raisins
4 cardamoms
1 teaspoon white peppercorns
½ cup anise seed
4 cups water
1 cup milk
½ to 1 cup sweetener

Blanch the pistachios and almonds. Soak the raisins, cardamoms and peppercorns for about a half hour. In a separate bowl, soak the anise seed for a half hour. Drain all these ingredients and put in a blender with the water.

Blend well at high speed, and then pour into a deep bowl. Strain liquid through muslin and discard the residue.

Add milk and sweetener to taste to the strained liquid. Mix well and chill. Serves 6.

SUPERSHAKE

½ cup powdered milk
2 teaspoons soy powder
1 teaspoon wheat germ
1 teaspoon brewer's yeast
1 teaspoon lecithin
1 teaspoon sesame butter
4 to 6 cashews
¼ cup sunflower seeds
2 tablespoons unsulphured molasses
2 tablespoons honey
1/3 cup water
½ banana, or 6 strawberries, or ½ peach or other
fresh fruit in season
2 tablespoons shredded coconut
8 ice cubes

Place nuts and seeds in a blender and grind. Add other ingredients and blend. Add ice cubes and blend until ice is broken up and drink is frothy. A real energy booster. Serves 1 or 2.

Variation:
Other ingredients, such as carob, yogurt, etc. may be substituted for some of the above ingredients.

HOT APPLE DRINK

4 cups fresh apple juice
a few sprigs of mint leaves
½ teaspoon cinnamon
¼ teaspoon garam masala spice (from Indian food
  store)
juice of ¼ lemon

Cook all ingredients except the lemon until the flavors are blended. Put in a pitcher; add lemon juice, stir, and serve. Serves 4.

SPICED APPLE SHAKE

1 large apple, peeled and chopped
1 cup milk
2 tablespoons powdered milk
1 teaspoon vanilla
½ teaspoon ground cinnamon
¼ teaspoon ground nutmeg
¼ teaspoon allspice
2 to 3 ice cubes
1 tablespoon honey (optional)

Put apple and milk in blender and whip. Add powdered milk and whip until smooth. Add vanilla and spices; drop in ice cubes and whip until ice is chopped very small and drink is smooth and foamy. Add honey to taste. Serves 2.

Variation:
2 peaches may be substituted for the apple; 2 teaspoons of maple syrup may be used instead of honey.

QUICK BREAKFAST

1½ cups fresh orange juice
½ cup yogurt
3 tablespoons wheat germ
1 to 2 tablespoons honey (optional)

Put all ingredients in a blender and whip for 30 seconds. Serve immediately. Makes 1 glass.

WHIPPED BUTTERMILK

1½ cups heavy cream
6 cups buttermilk
½ teaspoon allspice
1½ teaspoons cinnamon
1½ teaspoons grated nutmeg
4 tablespoons fresh lemon juice
¼ cup sweetener (rice syrup, maple syrup, powdered
  sugar)
grated rind of 1 lemon (optional)

Whip cream until almost stiff; set aside. Whip buttermilk until frothy. Add allspice, cinnamon, nutmeg, lemon juice and sweetener. Mix in the whipped cream and rind quickly. Chill. Pour into glasses and garnish with lemon slice, if desired. Serves 6.

ORANGE-APRICOT NECTAR

3 cups fresh orange juice
1½ cups apricot juice
1 cup grapefruit juice
4 tablespoons lemon juice
honey to taste

Combine all ingredients in a blender and whip until frothy. Serves 4.

STRAWBERRY-PINEAPPLE MILK

3 cups milk
1 pint strawberries, hulled
1 cup fresh pineapple chunks
3 tablespoons honey
1/8 teaspoon ground cardamom

Mix all ingredients in blender until smooth and creamy. Chill and serve. Serves 4.

Variation:
Add a scoop of ice cream to each glass.

BANANA-CANTALOUPE SMOOTHIE

1 cup milk
1 ripe banana, peeled
1/8 medium-size cantaloupe
1 teaspoon honey

Blend slowly in electric blender for 10 seconds and then for 30 more seconds at the highest speed. Serves 1.

ORANGE-BANANA FLIP

2 cups fresh-squeezed orange juice
1 large banana
4 ice cubes

Put ingredients in a blender and whip until well mixed and frothy. Serves 2.

RASPBERRY MILK

2 cups milk
1 cup fresh raspberries, cleaned
4 tablespoons powdered milk
½ teaspoon vanilla
2 teaspoons honey

Blend ingredients slowly in blender until milk powder is dissolved. Then whip at high speed for 1 minute. Serves 2.

PINEAPPLE-PARSLEY COOLER

10 ounces pineapple juice
1/3 cup fresh parsley
5 ice cubes

Put all ingredients into a blender and chop. Then increase to high speed until drink is light green and frothy. Serve immediately. Serves 4-6.

YOGURT DELIGHT

2 cucumbers
2 cups yogurt
juice of 1 lime
¾ to 1 teaspoon salt
¼ teaspoon black pepper
6 ice cubes

Peel cucumbers and remove the seeds; chop and put in blender. Add yogurt and lime juice and blend. Add spices to taste. Add ice cubes and whip until ice is crushed and spices are well combined. Serve immediately. Serves 4-6.

BUTTERMILK COOLER

2 cups buttermilk
½ cup fresh raspberries
½ cup fresh sliced strawberries
1 tablespoon honey

Blend raspberries and strawberries with about half of the buttermilk and the honey until smooth.

Divide mixture in two glasses and fill to the top with remaining buttermilk. Stir with spoon and serve. Serves 2.

YOGURT SHAKE

1 cup yogurt
1½ to 2 teaspoons honey
about 1 cup fresh strawberries, sliced
¼ teaspoon vanilla extract

Put all ingredients in a blender and whip until smooth and creamy. Serves 2.

Variation:

In place of strawberries, substitute other fresh fruit such as peaches, blueberries, raspberries, apricots, pineapple, nectarines, etc.

HOT APPLE CIDER

1 gallon apple cider
1 cup brown sugar or other sweetener to taste
1 cup lemon juice
4 cups fresh orange juice
1 lemon, thinly sliced
1 orange, thinly sliced
1 tablespoon whole cloves
1 tablespoon whole allspice
¼ piece of whole nutmeg
6 cinnamon sticks

Combine cider, sugar, juices and fruit in a large pan. Tie spices in cheesecloth and simmer in liquid for about 20 minutes.

Remove spice bag and serve cider while hot. Serves 18-24.

CRANBERRY PUNCH

1 cup raw almonds
½ cup hazelnuts
1 cup raisins or currants
1 apple, chopped
peel from 2 oranges
peel from ½ lemon
1 teaspoon whole cloves
½ teaspoon whole allspice
1 stick cinnamon
1 quart water
2 quarts cranberry juice
1 quart pineapple juice
2 cups orange juice

Put nuts, raisins, apple and peel in saucepan. Tie spices in cheesecloth and place in pan. Cover ingredients with water and simmer for about 15 minutes. Cool liquid and discard the spice bag.

Combine juices with cooled mixture and stir well. Serve hot or cold. Serves 18-24.

215

AMBROSIA

4 ripe bananas
½ cup fresh orange juice
¼ cup fresh coconut milk
¼ teaspoon almond extract
4 cups cold milk
honey to taste
whipped cream
fresh flaked coconut

In blender, beat bananas, orange juice, coconut milk and extract until well blended. Add milk and beat well. Add honey, stir, and pour into tall glasses. Garnish with whipped cream sprinkled with coconut. Serves 6.

Other
GoodThings

BANANAS FOR BABY

1 small banana, mashed
3 fresh strawberries
1 tablespoon yogurt

Mash fruit together and add yogurt to the desired consistency. Makes about 1 cup.

BABY FRUIT

12 fresh apricots, pitted, or 8 dried apricots
2 apples
2 pears

Peel and chop apricots. (If using dried apricots, steam for 2 to 3 minutes in just enough water to cover.) Peel and core apples and pears. Put all fruit in a blender and blend until smooth and creamy. Makes about 3 cups.

BABY'S SQUASH

¼ acorn or butternut squash
about 1 tablespoon milk
dab of butter
mild cheese, grated

Peel squash, discard seeds and cut into chunks. Put in steamer basket in a saucepan with about 1 inch of water. Cover and steam for about 20 minutes or until soft. Mash squash with milk to make squash smooth and creamy; add a dash of butter and a little grated cheese. Stir again and serve. Makes about 1 cup.

CHILDREN'S CHEESE SNACK

1 cup whole wheat flour
1 cup grated chedder cheese, or cottage cheese
¾ cup melted butter

Mix all ingredients and knead for a few minutes. Shape into small balls, flatten and bake in a moderate oven (350°) for about 30 minutes. Makes about 1 dozen.

YUMMY SPINACH FOR CHILDREN

½ pound fresh spinach, chopped
¼ carrot, grated
milk
½ cup cooked rice
2 tablespoons crumbled tofu

Fill sauce pan with chopped spinach and grated carrot. Add about ½ inch of milk to the pan. Bring milk to a boil; reduce heat; cook until milk "disappears." (Be careful not to let milk burn.) Add rice and tofu. Serve warm. Makes about 1 cup.

Variation:
    1/3 cup of peeled, chopped zucchini may be added or substituted.

BIRCHERMUS

3 tablespoons oatmeal
3 tablespoons apple juice or cold water
2 cups shredded apples
2 bananas, sliced
1 pint fresh strawberries, sliced
2 tablespoons finely chopped nuts
grated peel of 1 lemon (optional)
1 tablespoon lemon juice
½ cup chilled whipping cream
1 cup yogurt or sour cream
honey

Soak oatmeal in apple juice at least 3 hours. Drain and toss with apples, bananas, strawberries, nuts, lemon peel and juice.

Beat cream in chilled bowl until stiff. Fold whipped cream and yogurt into fruit. Sweeten to taste with honey. Garnish with additional fruit. Serves 4.

Variation: For a low calorie version, omit whipping cream and increase yogurt to 1½ cups.

221

RAISIN-CHEESE BREAKFAST CAKE

¼ cup butter
1 egg
2 tablespoons grated lemon peel
2 cups whole wheat pastry flour
3 tablespoons baking powder
½ teaspoon salt
2/3 cup milk or 1/3 cup milk + 1/3 cup yogurt
1 cup raisins
1 cup crumbled homemade cheese (recipe p. 6) or
any soft, mild, white cheese
2 tablespoons whole wheat pastry flour

Cream butter and egg. Add all but the last three ingredients and mix well. Dust raisins and cheese with 2 tablespoons flour. Fold into batter.
Pour into greased and floured 8 or 9 inch pan. Bake at
400° for 25 minutes. While still hot, make holes throughout
with a toothpick. Pour topping over cake and allow to soak
through. Serves 4-6.

TOPPING

½ cup butter
½ teaspoon ground cinnamon
½ teaspoon ground cardamom
¼ cup honey

In a small pan, melt butter with cinnamon and cardamom. When melted, stir into honey and whip with electric
mixer until smooth.

YOGURT WAFFLES

3 eggs, separated
½ cup yogurt
½ cup milk
¼ cup melted butter
1½ cups sifted whole wheat pastry flour
3 tablespoons baking powder
½ teaspoon salt
1 teaspoon rice syrup or fructose (optional)

Beat egg yolks, yogurt, milk and melted butter. Sift and add flour, baking powder and salt. Add rice syrup. Beat egg whites until stiff, but not dry, and fold into batter. Bake in a hot waffle iron. Serve with Pumpkin Butter (recipe follows). Makes about 8 waffles.

Note: These waffles make a good base for fruits, ice cream, creamed vegetables, etc.

PUMPKIN BUTTER

½ cup butter
½ cup cooked pumpkin
2 tablespoons light honey

Cream butter in mixer, gradually adding pumpkin and honey. Makes about 1 cup.

STRAWBERRY CREPES

1 tablespoon dry yeast
1 cup warm water
½ cup whole wheat flour
1 egg
1 tablespoon clarified butter
1 tablespoon raw sugar, date sugar or fructose
½ cup wheat germ
2 cups quartered fresh strawberries

Sprinkle yeast over warm water in a mixing bowl; stir well and beat in ½ cup whole wheat flour. Let stand in a warm place overnight.

In the morning add egg, butter, sweetener and wheat germ. Mix well and let stand a few minutes. Then cook like pancakes on a slightly oiled grill.

Fill with strawberries, roll up and serve with syrup, fresh cream or honey of roses (recipe follows). Makes 10-12 crepes.

HONEY OF ROSES

2 cups freshly gathered rose petals, unsprayed
1 cup water
1 tablespoon lemon juice
1 cup raw honey

Put rose petals in a heavy pan and cover with 1 cup water. Bring to a boil and simmer over low heat for 5 to 8 minutes. Strain and mix with lemon juice and honey. Serve over strawberry crepes. Makes about 4 cups.

GINGERBREAD WAFFLES

¼ cup butter
¼ cup rice syrup, fructose or date sugar
½ cup molasses
2 eggs, separated
1 cup milk or ½ cup milk + ½ cup yogurt
2¼ cups sifted whole wheat pastry flour
1½ teaspoons baking powder
1 teaspoon cinnamon
1 teaspoon ground ginger
¼ teaspoon ground cloves
¼ teaspoon salt
½ teaspoon ground cardamom (optional)

Beat together butter, rice syrup, molasses, egg yolks and milk. Stir in dry ingredients and mix well. Beat egg whites until stiff, but not dry. Fold into batter. Bake on hot waffle iron. Top with whipped cream or ice cream or Lemon Sauce (recipe follows). Makes about 12 waffles.

LEMON SAUCE

3 eggs
½ cup rice syrup, fructose or date sugar
juice of 1 lemon
2 tablespoons butter
dash of salt

Blend ingredients well. Cook in the top of a double boiler over simmering water for 15 minutes or until slightly thickened. Serve hot or cold. Makes about 1 cup.

SUNFLOWER MILLET PANCAKES

½ cup sunflower seeds
½ cup millet seeds
1 tablespoon dry yeast
½ cup water
1 tablespoon molasses

Cover seeds with water and let stand overnight. Put yeast and ½ cup water in a small bowl, cover, and leave overnight in a cool place.

The next morning, put the seeds and water through a blender. Add the yeast mixture and molasses; mix together. If the batter seems too thin, add a little flour to thicken. Set the bowl in a pan of warm water so it will rise quickly.

When double in bulk, stir again and fry on a griddle. Makes about 8 pancakes.

INDIAN PANCAKES
(Dosa)

1 cup raw rice
½ cup urad dahl (available from Indian food store)
1½ teaspoons salt
1/8 to ¼ teaspoon cayenne (optional)
water
½ cup yogurt
clarified butter

Soak the rice and dahl overnight, or for at least 6 hours. Drain. Blend in an electric blender with the salt and cayenne and add just enough water to blend well.

Pour into a bowl and add the yogurt. The batter should be like pancake batter. Thin with water if necessary.

Heat an iron skillet and grease with clarified butter. Pour about ¼ cup of batter into the skillet and spread very thin to the edge of the skillet. The batter will bubble on top when the underside is ready. Turn pancake over and brown for a few minutes on the other side.

Serve with a chutney (recipes pp. 240-241). Makes about 12-18 pancakes.

SCRAMBLED TOFU

1 small onion, grated
½ teaspoon turmeric
1 teaspoon cumin
1½ teaspoons coriander
2 tablespoons clarified butter
3 cups tofu, crumbled (recipe p. 8)
½ cup homemade cheese (recipe p. 6)
1 to 2 teaspoons salt (or to taste)
½ teaspoon tamari sauce
1 tablespoon lemon juice, fresh squeezed
2 tablespoons brewer's yeast (optional)

Fry the onion and spices in butter until nicely roasted. Add the tofu and cheese, stirring to coat with the spices. Add the remaining ingredients and allow the mixture to steam in its own juice until light and fluffy. If needed, add a tablespoon or two of hot water. Serve with whole wheat bread. Makes about 4 servings.

WHEAT SNACK
(Upma)

3 tablespoons clarified butter
½ teaspoon turmeric
½ teaspoon cayenne
1 teaspoon black mustard seed
¼ teaspoon ground cumin
½ teaspoon coriander
½ cup fresh peas
½ green pepper, chopped
½ cup chopped scallions
2 cups water
2 teaspoons salt
1 cup cream of wheat
juice of 1 lemon

In a saucepan, heat 2 tablespoons of the clarified butter. Add turmeric, cayenne, mustard seed, cumin and coriander and stir well. Fry until the mustard seed begins to pop. Then add peas, pepper and scallions. Stir well, coating the vegetables. Add the water and the salt.

Boil well, uncovered, for about 15 to 20 minutes or until the vegetables are tender and the water has cooked down. Then add the cream of wheat, lemon juice and 1 tablespoon of clarified butter.

Stir constantly and vigorously for 5 minutes. Do not permit the wheat to stick to the pan.

Serve the snack hot or cold, with any meal, or as a snack. Serves 6.

BABA GANOOSH

3 medium eggplants (dark in color)
2 cloves garlic
juice of 2 large lemons
½ cup tahini
salt
ground cumin to taste
½ cup yogurt

Puncture eggplants in several places with a fork; broil until black. Scoop out pulp and drain. Beat pulp. (If the eggplant is well done, the pulp can be beaten with a fork. Otherwise, use a blender.)

Press garlic and add to eggplant. Stir in tahini, salt and ¾ of the lemon juice. Stir thoroughly. Balance the taste with more lemon juice and tahini, if needed. Stir in a few pinches of cumin and the yogurt. Serve cold. Serves 4-6.

HOMUS

3 tablespoons sesame seed
1 cup chick peas, soaked overnight in 3 cups water
2 tablespoons clarified butter or sesame oil
3 tablespoons lemon juice
1 clove garlic, minced or 1 small onion, minced
¾ teaspoon salt
1/8 teaspoon pepper
¼ teaspoon ground cumin
½ cup tahini

In a small skillet, toast sesame seeds over medium heat until golden, shaking the pan often; set aside. Place remaining ingredients in a blender and combine until smooth. Add sesame seeds; blend. Chill.

Spoon into a small bowl and sprinkle with parsley. Serve with raw vegetables cut in bite-size pieces and wedges of pita bread. Makes about 1½ cups.

GUACAMOLE

1 ripe avocado, peeled and mashed
1 green onion, finely chopped
½ large green pepper, minced
1 tomato, peeled and chopped
1 sprig parsley, chopped
1 tablespoon cold pressed oil
½ tablespoon lemon or lime juice
pinch of salt
pinch of ground coriander
chili powder to taste

Combine ingredients in an electric blender or with a potato masher. Delicious with pita bread, as a dip, or as a sandwich on whole wheat bread. Makes about 1½ to 2 cups.

TOFU-AVOCADO SUPERSANDWICH

1½ teaspoons clarified butter
1 teaspoon turmeric
½ teaspoon ground cumin
¾ teaspoon ground coriander
1 tablespoon raw sunflower seeds
4 ounces tofu
salt, pepper and onion powder to taste
fresh yogurt
1 ripe avocado
1/8 teaspoon fresh-squeezed lemon juice
whole wheat bread
fresh alfalfa sprouts
1 tomato, peeled and sliced
lettuce

In a small frying pan stir-fry butter, turmeric, cumin and coriander over medium heat for about 1 minute. Add the sunflower seeds; fry for about 2 more minutes. Add the tofu while continuing to stir, and mash slightly with a fork. Add salt, pepper and onion power as desired. Add 1 to 2 tablespoons yogurt, stir in briefly, and remove from heat.

Mash avocado with a fork. Add the tofu mixture and stir together while adding lemon juice. Spread on whole grain, buttered toast. Add alfalfa sprouts, tomato and lettuce to make a very delicious sandwich. Spread will make 4 to 6 sandwiches.

"SHORT ORDER" TOFU LUNCHEON

1 tofu cake
about 1 tablespoon tamari or soy sauce
1 tablespoon clarified butter
whole grain bread
mayonnaise (recipe p. 128)
tomato slices
alfalfa sprouts

Cut a tofu cake into slices ¼ to 3/8 inch thick. In a small flat-bottomed bowl marinate the slices of tofu in tamari sauce for at least five minutes. Use about a teaspoon of tamari per slice. Turn the tofu in the sauce so both sides are flavored.

Then grill the tofu briefly in a little butter, turning once so that the slices are lightly browned.

Serve on whole grain bread or toast, a little mayonnaise, perhaps a slice of tomato and alfalfa sprouts.

BANANA FREEZE

10 frozen bananas (frozen without skins)
1½ cups sliced strawberries
½ cup whipping cream
¼ to ½ teaspoon vanilla

Put frozen bananas through a Champion juicer or puree in a blender or food processor until mashed, but still frozen. Return to the freezer again until serving time, if necessary, as bananas should be kept frozen.

Whip cream and vanilla. Add sliced strawberries as a topping to the frozen banana mixture and add a dollop of the whipped cream. No extra sweetener is needed. Serves about 6.

CARDAMOM ICE CREAM

4 eggs
1 cup honey
1 teaspoon vanilla
4 cups whipping cream
4 cups whole milk
2 tablespoons ground cardamom
½ to 1 cup pistachios, finely chopped

Cream eggs and honey. Add other ingredients, except nuts, and mix well. Taste for sweetness and seasoning. Stir in nuts.

Place into ice cream freezer and follow manufacturer's directions. Makes just over ½ gallon.

PAPAYA CIRCLES

2 papayas
1 cup homemade cheese (recipe p. 6) or any soft, mild, white cheese
½ cup yogurt cheese, kefir cheese or cream cheese
1 tablespoon honey
dash of salt
2 tablespoons lemon juice

Cut off the top of papayas about ¼ of the way down. Carefully scoop out seeds so as not to spoil the shape of the opening.

Combine homemade cheese, yogurt cheese, honey, salt and lemon juice in blender. Blend until smooth. Pack mixture into core of papaya. Chill 1 to 2 hours or until center is firm.

With very sharp knife or vegetable peeler, carefully peel the papaya. Slice into 1-inch circles. Serve alone, as part of a fruit plate, or as a snack. Serves 4.

BANANA YOGURT CREAM

2 cups yogurt
1 teaspoon clarified butter
1 teaspoon cumin seed
seed from one cardamom pod, ground
1 teaspoon salt
¼ teaspoon cayenne
2 ripe bananas

Whip yogurt in mixing bowl. Fry cumin and cardamom in the butter. When cumin begins to brown, add salt and cayenne. Mash bananas well and add to the spices in the pan. Quickly add the yogurt, stir well and remove from heat. Chill and serve in bowls with dinner. Serves 4.

INDIAN SILK

1 quart yogurt
1 cup raw sugar
1 teaspoon rosewater
seed from one cardamom pod, ground
½ teaspoon ground nutmeg
¼ teaspoon crumbled saffron threads

Place yogurt in a square of fine muslin and hang over the sink to drain. Let drain for twelve hours.

Rubber band another piece of muslin firmly to a large, heavy bowl. Put half of the yogurt and half of the sugar in the muslin. Work the yogurt and sugar through the muslin into the bowl. Do the same with the remaining yogurt and sugar. (The fine, silky consistency of the dish requires use of muslin in this way.)

Remove the muslin, taking care to scrape the bottom of the muslin. Add the rosewater, cardamom, nutmeg and saffron to the yogurt. Stir well. Chill and serve. Serves 6.

239

TOMATO CHUTNEY

½ onion, chopped
a few sprigs of fresh green coriander
4 tomatoes, without skins
1 teaspoon salt
1 teaspoon pepper
¼ teaspoon red pepper

Put all ingredients in a blender and blend until a thick liquid consistency. Makes 2 cups.

TOMATO MINT CHUTNEY

4 tomatoes, peeled
2 apples, peeled and cored
2 handfuls fresh mint
¼ to ½ teaspoon cayenne pepper
1 teaspoon salt
juice of 1 lemon

Put all ingredients in a blender and blend until smooth. If consistency is thin, add more apple. Makes about 2 cups.

COCONUT CHUTNEY

1 cup fresh coconut
2 tablespoons chopped fresh ginger root
¼ teaspoon chili powder
1 teaspoon salt
1 teaspoon sugar
juice of 1 lemon
water

Blend the coconut and spices with enough water to chop the coconut very fine. Add sugar and lemon juice. Let set for about 15 minutes and then pour off the water until the desired consistency is reached. Makes about 2 cups.

SESAME SEED CHUTNEY

1 cup sesame seed
¼ cup water
1 chili pepper, chopped
1 tablespoon fresh chopped ginger
1 teaspoon salt
juice of 1 lemon
1 tablespoon honey
pulp of 1 tomato

Blend all ingredients in blender until smooth. Makes about 2 cups.

FRUIT CANDY

2 cups boiling water
¾ cup dried apricots
½ cup dried pineapple
½ cup dried apples
½ cup pitted prunes
1¼ cup pitted dates
1 cup raisins
¾ cup dried currants
1 cup walnuts
½ cup pecans
½ cup hazelnuts
½ cup brazil nuts
soft butter
fresh shredded coconut

Pour boiling water over apricots and pineapple. Let stand for half an hour. Drain fruit. In a large bowl combine the fruits and nuts and drop by handfuls into a food chopper. Butter hands; form fruit/nut mixture into small balls and roll in coconut. Chill, if desired. Makes about 24 balls.

Index

243

249

The main building of the national headquarters, Honesdale, Pa.

The Himalayan Institute

The Himalayan International Institute of Yoga Science and Philosophy of the U.S.A. is a nonprofit organization devoted to the scientific and spiritual progress of modern man. Founded in 1971 by Sri Swami Rama, the Institute combines Western and Eastern teachings and techniques to develop educational, therapeutic, and research programs for serving people in today's world. The goals of the Institute are to teach meditational techniques for the growth of individuals and their society, to make known the harmonious view of world religions and philosophies, and to undertake scientific research for the benefit of humanity.

This challenging task is met by people of all ages, all walks of life, and all faiths who attend and participate in the Institute courses and seminars. These programs, which are given on a continuing basis, are designed in order that one may discover for oneself how to live more creatively. In the words of Swami Rama, "By being aware of one's own potential and abilities, one can become a perfect citizen, help the nation, and serve humanity."

The Institute has branch centers and affiliates throughout the United States. The 422-acre campus of the national headquarters located in the Pocono Mountains of northeastern Pennsylvania, serves as the coordination center for all the Institute activities, which include a wide variety of innovative programs in education, research, and therapy, combining Eastern and Western approaches to self-awareness and self-directed change.

SEMINARS, LECTURES, PROGRAMS, and CLASSES are available throughout the year, providing intensive training and experience in such topics as Superconscious Meditation, hatha yoga, philosophy, psychology, and various aspects of personal growth and holistic health. The *Himalayan News,* a free bimonthly publication, provides a complete listing, description, and schedule of courses.

The RESIDENTIAL and SELF-TRANSFORMATION PROGRAMS provide training in the basic yoga disciplines—diet, ethical behavior, hatha yoga, and meditation. Students are also given guidance in a philosophy of living in a community environment.

The PROGRAM IN EASTERN STUDIES AND COMPARATIVE PSYCHOLOGY is the first curriculum offered by an educational institution that provides a systematic synthesis of Western empirical sciences with Eastern introspective sciences using both practical and traditional approaches to education. The University of Scranton, by an agreement of affiliation with the Himalayan Institute, is prepared to grant credits for coursework in this program, and upon successful completion of the program awards a Master of Science degree.

The five-day STRESS MANAGEMENT/PHYSICAL FITNESS PROGRAM offers practical and individualized training that can be used to control the stress response. This includes biofeedback, relaxation skills, exercise, diet, breathing techniques, and meditation.

A yearly INTERNATIONAL CONGRESS, sponsored by the Institute, is devoted to the scientific and spiritual progress of modern man. Through lectures, workshops, seminars, and practical demonstrations, it provides a forum for professionals and laymen to share their knowledge and research.

The ELEANOR N. DANA RESEARCH LABORATORY is the psychophysiological laboratory of the Institute, specializing in research on breathing, meditation, holistic therapies, and stress and relaxed states. The laboratory is fully equipped for exercise stress testing and psychophysiological measurements, including brain waves, patterns of respiration, heart rate changes, and muscle tension. The staff investigates Eastern teachings through studies based on Western experimental techniques.

Himalayan Institute Publications

Choosing a Path	Swami Rama
Living with the Himalayan Masters	Swami Rama
A Practical Guide to Holistic Health	Swami Rama
Freedom from the Bondage of Karma	Swami Rama
Book of Wisdom	Swami Rama
Lectures on Yoga	Swami Rama
Life Here and Hereafter	Swami Rama
Marriage, Parenthood, and Enlightenment	Swami Rama
Emotion to Enlightenment	Swami Rama, Swami Ajaya
Science of Breath	Swami Rama, Rudolph Ballentine, M.D., Alan Hymes, M.D.
Yoga and Psychotherapy	Swami Rama, Rudolph Ballentine, M.D., Swami Ajaya
Superconscious Meditation	Usharbudh Arya, D.Litt.
Mantra and Meditation	Usharbudh Arya, D.Litt.
Philosophy of Hatha Yoga	Usharbudh Arya, D.Litt.
Meditation and the Art of Dying	Usharbudh Arya, D.Litt.
God	Usharbudh Arya, D.Litt.
Yoga Psychology	Swami Ajaya
Foundations of Eastern and Western Psychology	Swami Ajaya (ed.)
Psychology East and West	Swami Ajaya (ed.)
Meditational Therapy	Swami Ajaya (ed.)
Diet and Nutrition	Rudolph Ballentine, M.D.
Joints and Glands Exercises	Rudolph Ballentine, M.D. (ed.)
Theory and Practice of Meditation	Rudolph Ballentine, M.D. (ed.)
Art and Science of Meditation	L. K. Misra, Ph.D. (ed.)
Freedom from Stress	Phil Nuernberger, Ph.D.
Yoga and Christianity	Justin O'Brien, D.Th.
Science Studies Yoga	James Funderburk, Ph.D.
Homeopathic Remedies	Drs. Anderson, Buegel, Chernin
Hatha Yoga Manual I	Samskrti and Veda
Hatha Yoga Manual II	Samskrti and Judith Franks
Swami Rama of the Himalayas	L. K. Misra, Ph.D. (ed.)
Philosophy of Death and Dying	M. V. Kamath
Practical Vedanta of Swami Rama Tirtha	Brandt Dayton (ed.)
Sanskrit without Tears	S. N. Agnihotri, Ph.D.
Psychology of the Beatitudes	Arpita
Himalayan Mountain Cookery	Martha Ballentine
The Yoga Way Cookbook	Himalayan Institute
Inner Paths	Himalayan Institute
Meditation in Christianity	Himalayan Institute
Faces of Meditation	Himalayan Institute
Therapeutic Value of Yoga	Himalayan Institute
Chants from Eternity	Himalayan Institute
Thought for the Day	Himalayan Institute
Spiritual Diary	Himalayan Institute
Blank Books	Himalayan Institute